Floriana Petersen

111 Places in San Francisco That You Must Not Miss

Photographs by Steve Werney

111

emons:

Many San Franciscans shared their city secrets with us for this book. Special thanks are due to Barbara Roether and Mark MacNamara, who contributed not only suggestions but history, background, and literary inspiration. — F.P.

© Bibliographical information of the Deutsche Nationalbibliothek
The Deutsche Nationalbibliothek lists this publication in the Deutsche Nationalbibliografie; detailed bibliographical data are available on the internet at http://dnb.d-nb.de.

MIX
Paper | Supporting responsible forestry
FSC® C177064

Cäcilienstraße 48, 50667 Köln
info@emons-verlag.de

Edited by Katrina Fried
Design: Eva Kraskes, based on a design
by Lübbeke | Naumann | Thoben
Maps: altancicek.design, www.altancicek.de
Printing and binding: sourc-e GmbH
Printed in Europe 2025
ISBN 978-3-7408-2882-0
First edition 2016
Revised 13th edition, December 2025

Guidebooks for Locals & Experienced Travelers
Join us in uncovering new places around the world at
www.111places.com

Foreword

In all my years living in San Francisco, I have never stopped discovering new places, hidden stairways, unexpected vistas, and stories embedded in every crevice. Strolling the city's rolling terrain brings you face-to-face with these charming details, like the scrollwork on an old Victorian, an overgrown garden of jasmine in a concealed alley, or the lively salsa rhythms drifting out of an open window.

For a city that is only seven miles wide and seven miles long, the diversity here is stunning; from musicians, artists, and hippies, to hipsters and entrepreneurs, its population reflects every human shape, color, and spirit. It's not only the people who have defined the neighborhoods, but the land itself: there are 14 hills across which the city rises and falls.

In San Francisco, each hill, from Telegraph to Potrero, and every valley, from Noe to Hayes, has its own architecture, its own history, and even its own weather. Visitors often find it hard to comprehend that the sunny blue skies of the Mission District turn to cold and fog just over Twin Peaks. Locals know to dress for the many microclimates, and expect the sudden shifts in temperature. In many ways, extremes are in the DNA of San Francisco, a notion that becomes ever clearer as you delve into the city's storied past. During the Gold Rush, the population went from around 1,000 in 1848 to 30,000 in 1850; and by 1855, almost 300,000 people lived here. For decades San Francisco was the only outpost of real civilization west of the Rockies. 1848 may seem new by European standards, but for the American West, this is the old mother city.

All cities change; the recent boom in Silicon Valley has made the Bay Area a new playground for young millionaires. People, and wealth, come and go quickly here, but the landscape – the purple headlands jutting into the Pacific, the island-scattered bay, the fog pouring over the Golden Gate Bridge – is as stoic and enduring as Nature itself.

111 Places

IN MEMORY OF
OUR BELOVED
FRITZ
SGT. HAYFORD
1956 — 1961

1 140 New Montgomery

It's all about communication

The Pacific Telephone Building rose up at 140 Montgomery Street to be San Francisco's first skyscraper. It was built in 1925 for $4 million and provided offices for 2,000 workers, mostly women. With its fresh look of verticality and its Art Deco lobby, including the reddish ceiling full of unicorns, phoenixes, and clouds, the building suggested a new style of workplace. Dressed in highly reflective, granite-colored terra-cotta exterior panels, it presided over the city for 40 years.

The architect was Timothy Pflueger (1892–1946), a San Francisco native, who – in the wake of the 1906 earthquake – never went to college yet found his way to the field of architecture and interior design. Following Prohibition, Pflueger's interiors graced the city's most renowned cocktail lounges, most notably the Patent Leather Bar at the St. Francis Hotel. Other well-known Pflueger buildings include the Castro and Alhambra theaters (see ch. 4), and 450 Sutter street. He also designed buildings for the Olympic Club, the quintessential West Coast men's club, of which he, himself, was a member. One night, after his customary swim, he dropped dead from a heart attack on the street outside.

Pflueger's inspiration for 140 Montgomery was a never-built skyscraper imagined by the great Finnish architect, Gottlieb Eliel Saarinen. Now, almost 90 years after it was built, the 26-story building is lost in the glass-and-steel forest that has grown around it. Yet it remains not only an architectural landmark, but also a symbol of the city's focus on communications: Pacific Telephone was a cutting-edge company in its day. The building's main client now is Yelp, the online review site. Today, the interior includes various "perks" typical of the modern, progressive, start-up workplace culture, such as showers for commuters and a bike repair shop built inside a former wood-paneled boardroom.

Address 140 New Montgomery Street, San Francisco, CA 94105 | Getting there Bus: 8X (3rd St & Howard St stop); 10, 12 (2nd St & Howard St stop) | Tip Beautiful restaurant Mourad, located in the same building at 140 Montgomery, offers modern variation of Marrocan cuisine.

2 826 Valencia

Reading, writing, and "Ahoy, matey!"

This city is full of creative characters and always has been, and writer Dave Eggers is among the most honorable examples. Eggers is a genuine renaissance fellow, a Bono of words, whose 2000 blockbuster memoir, *A Heartbreaking Work of Staggering Genius*, became a way to parlay his literary wits and profits into various collaborations, some of which involve methods for teaching kids how to read and write and teachers how to inspire their students.

In 2002 Eggers teamed up with educator and advocate Nínive Calegari to organize a one-on-one tutoring program for kids. He found a location at 826 Valencia Street, which in those days was in a "shopping-hood" with retro furniture stores and a Santeria shop. The idea was to run his quarterly literary magazine and publishing company, McSweeneys, out of the same building, and have his staff and community of writers and editors work with the neighborhood kids after school. From the start, the charter was to draw students into a space where imagination was king, and where writing was respected and explored.

To make it a going concern, Eggers and Calegari opened up a pirate-supply store in the front of the building, where you can pick up practically anything an aspiring or practicing swashbuckler might need – from peg legs and mermaid bait (or repellant), to eye patches and planks sold by the foot. Although the shop was created as a means to an end, it is an enchantment in its own right, not to mention a terrific magnet for potential pupils. After all, who wouldn't rather do their homework surrounded by pirate paraphernalia instead of at their kitchen table?

Incidentally, 826 Valencia has nonprofit extensions in seven other cities across the country. Programs for kids ages 6 to 18 include tutoring, publishing, and college and career training, along with parallel opportunities for teachers.

Address 826 Valencia Street, San Francisco, CA 94110, +1 415.642.905, www.826valencia.org | Getting there Bus: 33 (18th St & Valencia St stop) | Hours Mon–Fri 9:30am–6pm | Tip Stop at Dandelion Chocolate at 740 Valencia Street. You can sit in the front cafe and watch the chocolate-making process in the factory in the back.

3 1450 Noriega Street

Where the heiress robbed a bank

In the 1970s, the Outer Sunset District was an increasingly Asian suburb far removed from downtown. On the corner of Noriega and 22nd Avenue stands what was then a branch of the Hibernia Savings & Loan. At 10am on April 15, 1974, several members of a Marxist-inspired radical group known as the Symbionese Liberation Army (SLA) burst into the bank. While several revolutionaries gathered cash from the tellers, a young woman wearing a tilted beret and carrying an M-1 carbine shouted instructions to customers. A security camera caught an iconic photo of Patty Hearst, the granddaughter of publishing baron William Randolph Hearst. Coincidentally, one of Patty's close friends growing up was a daughter in the Tobin family, which founded the Hibernia Bank.

Ms. Hearst had been kidnapped nine weeks earlier, shortly before her 20th birthday, taken from a Berkeley apartment that she shared with her then fiancé. The next month during a botched theft in a Los Angeles sporting goods store, Ms. Hearst seemed to have completely shed her bourgeois upbringing and joined the SLA in earnest. She fired several shots to help her comrades escape; they were later tracked down and killed in one of the biggest shootouts in California history. A year later, Hearst served as the getaway driver in another bank robbery. One customer was shot to death. The following September, "Tanya," her nom de guerre, was arrested in San Francisco, and when asked her profession replied, "urban guerilla."

She was eventually tried for the Hibernia holdup, and, despite overwhelming evidence that she suffered from Stockholm syndrome, was found guilty of conspiracy and served 21 months in prison after her sentence was commuted. Eventually, President Clinton gave her a presidential pardon. Today, the former Hibernia branch on Noriega Street houses a medical services company and a Bank of America cash machine.

Address 1450 Noriega Street, San Francisco, CA 94122 | **Getting there** Bus: 16X, 71, 71L (22nd Ave & Noriega St stop) | **Tip** You can find inexpensive and tasty dim sum just down the block at New Hing Lung at 1556 Noriega Street.

4 Alhambra Theater

A cinematic workout

In the 1920s, elaborate movie palaces sprang up in cities across America, creating fantastical architectural wonders to match the fantasies of Hollywood. The Alhambra Theater on Polk Street, incorporating all the excesses of true Islamic design, was one of the city's finest examples. Designed by Timothy Pflueger in 1926, the Alhambra's iconic "minarets" originally glowed red to beckon viewers in to its 1,500 seats. After Charlie Chaplin had shuffled off, after Greta Garbo had whispered her final words, the lights would come up on the dreamy Arabian interior of the auditorium: horseshoe arches floating over sapphire-colored niches, a central dome decorated with a flower of arabesques, and filigree plasterwork trailing over everything.

In the 1960s, this neighborhood was the center of gay culture in San Francisco. The first openly gay business association in America, the Tavern Guild, was created by bar owners on Polk Street, which is still dominated by small storefront shops and cafes. When the gay scene shifted to the Castro District in the early seventies, the street fell on hard times. The Alhambra tried to keep its doors open by dividing the theater into two auditoriums, then briefly returned to a single screen again in the late eighties, but finally closed in 1998.

And yet, in the true spirit of *Arabian Nights*, or of happy Hollywood endings, the story of the Alhambra goes on. Since 2001, the theater has been home to Crunch Fitness, a popular gym. A careful restoration and conversion to workout space has retained most of the interior detail. The projection room has been reimagined as a yoga studio and the area behind the screen is now a spinning room. A second tier contains weights and machines, but in the balcony some thirteen original seats from the old theater remain.

Best of all, there is still a movie screen to watch as you stretch, sweat, and tone.

Address 2330 Polk Street, San Francisco, CA 94109 | Getting there Bus: 19 (Polk St & Union St stop) | Hours Mon–Fri 5am–10pm, Sat & Sun 7am–8pm | Tip With its little stores and delightful cafes, the north side of Polk Street is perfect for a window-shopping stroll.

5 Angel Island Immigration Station

Exclusion runs in the blood

The Chinese Exclusion Act of 1882, signed into law by America's "most forgotten president," Republican Chester Arthur, is a reminder that the United States has a long and sordid relationship with immigrants — not least with the Chinese laborers who were originally welcomed into America to build the 1,900-mile Transcontinental Railroad in the 1860s. The Chinese, originally thought to be physically unfit for the work, turned out to be tough, tenacious, and above all, efficient. At one point, tens of thousands of Chinese laborers prepared the land, bored tunnels, and laid track, working at a record setting pace, all for between $1 and $3 a day, much less than their white counterparts.

After building the railway, Chinese laborers found other work in agriculture and mining. But when the Gold Rush subsided and panning for gold lead to the more grueling and competitive business of mining for gold, along with the recession of 1870, the public began to resent cheap labor. A flurry of federal laws was passed to discourage Chinese immigration, particularly in California. In 1910, the Angel Island Immigration Station, also called the "West Coast Ellis Island," opened.

Once home to the coastal Miwok tribe, the 750-acre island in San Francisco Bay was used to slow 175,000 Chinese from entering the country between 1910 and 1940. The Chinese Exclusion Act was repealed in 1943. Perhaps the most striking testimonies are the 200 poems written on the detention center walls that have been restored. In 1963, the original detention center became a state park.

You reach Angel Island by small boat, kayak, or ferries from San Francisco, Tiburon, or Vallejo. Bicycles can be rented on the island, along with electric scooters and Segways.

Address Angel Island State Park, Angel Island, CA 94920, +1 415.435.5537, www.angelisland.org | Getting there Check the website for the ferry schedule | Hours Wed–Sat 11am–3pm | Tip If you camp there, note that charcoal grills and camp stoves are permitted, but no wood fires are allowed.

6 The Antique Vibrator Museum

A history of good vibrations

"Baghdad by the Bay," as longtime *Chronicle*columnist Herb Caen used to call San Francisco, has always been about pleasure. From the beginning, the city's character has been shaped by wealth, innovation, diversity, and a vague sense of permissiveness, an acceptance of the "queer and questioning" in every sense.

The hedonistic principles of the city have been defined by various movements, not least the "Sex Positive Movement," about which sexologist Dr. Carol Queen once noted, "'Sex-positive' respects each of our unique sexual profiles, even as we acknowledge that some of us have been damaged by a culture that tries to eradicate sexual difference and possibility." The term *sex positive* may have been coined by the Austrian psychoanalyst and "sex box" inventor, Wilhelm Reich, and took root in San Francisco in the 1960s and 1970s.

The spirit, practice, and technology of the Sex Positive Movement is best seen in the Antique Vibrator Museum, located in Good Vibrations, a sex shop oriented toward women. The shop opened in 1977; its ethos is eroticism, as opposed to pornography. You must be at least 18 to enter.

The museum, curated by Dr. Queen, opened in 2012 and consists of a medium-sized room with display cases showing the evolution of the electric vibrator from the 1800s to the present. The presentation is superb, and the history is amusing, evocative, and enlightening. Admission is free and you can also book a private tour with Dr. Queen. Many of the early machines look like classic eggbeaters or Betty Crocker mixers. What's interesting, of course, is that the technology grew out of a largely male conviction that women's sexual issues were linked to hysteria and that feminine sexuality was something to be feared as well as properly managed.

Address 1620 Polk Street, San Francisco, CA 94109, +1 415.345.0400, www.antiquevibratormuseum.com | Getting there Bus: 19 (Polk St & California St stop) | Hours Mon–Wed & Fri–Sun 12:30–6:30pm, Thu 12:30–7pm | Tip To continue your sensual experience, walk six blocks north to Les Cent Culottes to shop for some fine French lingerie (2200 Polk Street).

7 Arion Press

Lost and foundry

When real-life Citizen Kane, William Randolph Hearst, bought the *San Francisco Examiner* in 1887, it was his new state-of-the-art printing presses that helped "the Ex" become the "Monarch of the Dailies." Since then, innovative printers and publishers have been a critical force behind the city's cultural history. Arion Press and the Grabhorn Institute both preserve this legacy as well as insure its future.

Housed in a sprawling Presidio building, the center includes operating letterpress equipment, the bookbindery, and, most unique, the foundry of Mackenzie & Harris (M & H), which celebrated its 100th birthday in 2015 and is one of the last working metal type foundries in the world. Visitors can observe all this equipment still being used: type being cast from molten metal and set into pages; pages being printed on letterpresses and then hand sewn into blocks and bound onto boards and into cases. The artisans who work at Arion undergo years of apprenticeship, and are considered among the finest printers in the country.

Until the advent of desktop publishing, letterpress printing was the mainstay of the local literary scene, as writers and political activists seized the do-it-yourself potential of the small printing press. From storefronts and garages, in the Mission and Dogpatch, poet-printers churned out thousands of limited-run books and broadsides, often using M & H.

The foundry, and the 3,888 cases of metal type in its collection, might have been lost but for the foresight of Arion Press's founder, Andrew Hoyem, who helped create the Grabhorn Institute. Bibliophiles will appreciate the changing selection of Arion's fine hand-printed books, most famously among them *Moby Dick* and *Leaves of Grass*, which are on display in their gallery. Public demonstration tours are held Thursday afternoons at 3:30pm and last approximately an hour and a half.

Address 1802 Hays Street, The Presidio, San Francisco, CA 94129, +1 415.668.2542, www.arionpress.com | **Getting there** Bus: 1, 1 AX, 28 (California St & Park Presidio Blvd stop) | **Hours** Gallery, Mon–Fri 10am–5pm; visit the website for tour schedule | **Tip** A lovely little cafe nearby is Japonica on 5503 California Street.

8 The Audium

Seeing with your ears

Stan Shaff is a music composer who became drawn to the unexplored properties of sound, and in particular the way sound is affected by the space you hear it in. In the late 1950s, he collaborated with another professional musician, Doug McEachern, who was also an equipment engineer. The two began experimenting with recording technology, speaker systems, and architectural features to create a revolutionary setting where you could "experience" sound, not just listen to it.

From a composer's perspective, this new space, the Audium, is another tool for the making of "sound sculptures." But Shaff's intention, as it has evolved over the years, is in part to lead his audience to an understanding of the contradiction between the fast-moving world outside the Audium and the experience to be had inside. In this sense, sound can be a metaphysical encounter.

At the Audium's theater on Bush Street, performances are every Friday and Saturday night at 8:30pm. Shaff, himself, often takes tickets and leads people to their seats – there are only 49, set in concentric circles. When the first public performances began in 1960, there were 8 speakers; now there are 176, including ones installed under each seat. The compositions weave together sounds that are both familiar and strange – from music, nature, and the everyday – as you sit in absolute darkness.

Shaff has been quoted to say, "I have always been possessed by the evocative qualities all sounds seem to have, whether natural or electronic. Sounds touch deeper levels of our inner life, layers that lie just beneath the visual world ... Audiences should feel sound as it bumps up against them, caresses, travels through, covers and enfolds them. I ask listeners to see with their ears and feel with their bodies sounds as images, dreams and memories. As people walk into a work, they become part of its realization."

Address 1616 Bush Street, San Francisco, CA 94109, +1 415.771.1616, www.audium.org | Getting there Bus: 38 (Starr King Way St & Gough St stop) | Hours See website for schedule | Tip Stroll down the hidden brick pathway of the Historic Cottage Row bounded by Bush, Sutter, and Webster Streets, lined with quaint Victorians built during the late 1860s and 1870s. On the Sutter side is a pleasant mini park with benches.

9_ Balmy Alley Murals

Struggle and change

Up until a few years ago, when gentrification began setting in, residents of the mostly Latino Mission District considered Frida Kahlo their patron saint and Diego Rivera their artistic director. The Mexican mural movement that Rivera brought to the city in the 1930s had a second flowering here in the 1970s, and Balmy Alley was its center. Starting in 1972, a small group of Chicana artists, the Mujeres Muralistas, painted the first large works on the wooden garage doors and fences that abut this narrow residential alleyway. Their murals were political statements against conflict, but from a distinctly feminine perspective, depicting the transcendent power of the earth, women, children, and the cycles of nature. Thousands of immigrants fleeing civil unrest in Nicaragua, Salvador, and Guatemala settled in this neighborhood in the 1980s, and the murals reflected their struggles.

Each successive wave of residents has left an indelible artistic imprint on the alley. Recently restored, the painting titled *Culture Contains the Seed of Resistance that Blossoms into the Flower of Liberation* was one of 25 murals created in 1985. The iconic *Naya Bihana* (New Dawn) painted by Martin Travers in 2002, depicts the women of Nepal struggling to break the chains of oppression, the theme of so many of the murals here. The gentrification that began in the late nineties is also portrayed in various works, such as Lucia Ippolito's *Mission Makeover*, which depicts a day in the life of a Mission teenager who gets searched by a police officer drinking Starbucks coffee; or the fantastic *Victorion*, by Sirron Norris, in which a giant robot-like character made of Victorian houses is sent to crush the real-estate developers under his feet.

Not long ago, however, one of the larger apartment buildings was renovated; and the garage abutting the alley was clad in painted steel. A surveillance camera now discourages any new creative embellishments.

Address 1-100 Balmy Street, San Francisco, CA 94110 | **Getting there** Bus: 12, 14 (Mission St & 24th St stop); 48, 67 (Folsom St & 24th St stop) | **Tip** For an al fresco Mexican dining experience, treat yourself to a couple of tacos at the El Gallo Giro Taco Truck on Treat Street and 23rd Street.

10 The Battery

Old world, new school

San Francisco has long been a "clubby" town, with a distinctly blue-blazer sensibility. But today, less than a dozen of the private, elite, mostly male social clubs remain. Much like the San Francisco Symphony, as well as the ballet and the opera, these old-school clubs face the difficult challenge of replacing an aging clientele. As a result, some have relaxed their admittance policies, expanded entertainment programs, and even begun to use social media – all in an effort to attract an eclectic variety of members and capture the zeitgeist of the city.

Among a crop of new and innovative members-only clubs is the Battery, which opened in 2013. Membership is by referral only and dues are $2,400 a year. The Battery's vision "is to create a culture where inspiration is embraced, diverse communities come together and egos are checked at the door." Inside the old Musto building in Jackson Square, which was once a marble factory and then a candy warehouse, the club has created a retro-hipster playground tricked out with a gym, a spa, four bars, a restaurant, a library, a 20-person hot tub, a 3,000-square-foot wine cellar and an exclusive "inn" comprising just 14 rooms and a penthouse. The mood of the interior is reminiscent of a 21st-century Hearst Castle, with fresh, bright colors, faux finishes, comfy leather chairs, filled bookcases, and curious vintage objects.

The club also hosts inspiring exhibitions featuring up and coming local artists and monthly gallery tours. It's all a reflection of the cultural taste of owners and spouses Michael and Xochi Birch, who in 2008 sold their social networking company Bebo for a whopping $850 million.

If you can't score an invite from a member, you might consider splurging on one of the suites or guest rooms. Overnight visitors are regarded as "Resident Members" and are privy to many of the amenities and facilities the Battery has to offer.

Address 717 Battery Street, San Francisco CA 94111, www.thebatterysf.com | Getting there Bus: 10, 12 (Pacific Ave & Sansome St stop) | Hours By member-invitation only | Tip Just a couple blocks away in Jackson Square is the Hedge, a minimalistic gallery space at 501 Pacific Avenue.

11 The Bay Lights

The Bay Bridge gets its bling

The Oakland Bay Bridge, with its double deck, opened in November 1936, six months before the Golden Gate Bridge, and has always been considered the latter's ugly cousin. Then in 2013, the eastern span, from Treasure Island to Oakland, was recast into a great white swan of a bridge, and the western span – which offers a terrific view of the city from the top deck as you drive across – became the unlikely canvas for one of the most ambitious light sculptures ever made.

The man responsible for this luminescent face-lift is artist Leo Villareal. His work, which you'll find in such venerable institutions as the Museum of Modern Art in New York and the National Gallery in Washington, D.C., features LED lights, which are controlled through a custom-designed computer program.

In 2013, he transformed the north side of the bridge's drab countenance using 25,000 separate lights strung 12 inches apart along the vertical suspension cables. The lights appear to float up and down the cables as they blink on and off in randomized patterns. The effect this creates has a mesmerizing musical quality, as the installation blends in with the headlights of the bridge traffic and the high-rise windows of downtown San Francisco. It lends the entire waterfront a jewel-like ambience.

Electricity for the project costs about $30 a day and the lights can be set to different levels of brightness. The lights are visible from many angles along the waterfront from sunset until 2am, but are especially dazzling when viewed from the public deck behind the Ferry Building, on the Embarcadero. For safety reasons, the light show cannot be seen by motorists driving on the bridge.

The Bay Lights have become so popular that the installation will burn long past its original expiration date of 2015. Funds raised will transform the spectacle from temporary to permanent.

Address Pier 14, San Francisco, CA 94105, thebaylights.illuminatethearts.org | Getting there Light rail: T-Third, N-Judah (Embarcadero & Folsom St stop) | Hours The Bay Lights are lit sunset–2am | Tip Savoring oysters at Water Bar (399 Embarcadero) is the perfect complement to an enjoyable view of the Bay Lights.

12 The Beach & Park Chalet

Upstairs, downstairs, in Golden Gate Park

On the western border of San Francisco, at the Golden Gate Park waterfront, you'll find the Beach and Park Chalet, where locals are likely to spend a Saturday afternoon, or even a foggy evening, lounging on the chairs in back of a 100-year-old building that houses two restaurants. Upstairs, at the Beach Chalet, the special offering is a view of the coast across the Great Highway, while downstairs at the Park Chalet, life spills into the park itself. Kids can frolic among the trees while parents enjoy a microbrew and live music.

The building, Spanish colonial in design, was the work of Willis Polk, supervising architect of the Panama-Pacific Exposition of 1915. The Exposition was a celebration of the new canal but became a showcase for San Francisco's recovery from the earthquake in 1906. Polk's best work includes the Pacific Union Club, the Filoli Estate, the War Memorial Opera House, and the Hobart Building. It was also Polk who guided the restoration of Bernard Maybeck's Palace of Fine Arts and who said, "Make no small plans for they have not the power to stir men's minds."

Visitors entering the Beach Chalet are immediately struck by the superbly done wraparound murals comprising frescoes done in the Arts and Crafts style. Created by Lucien Labaudt, a self-taught French artist who came to the city in 1910, the murals offer an intimate sense of San Francisco during the Great Depression. The scenes are foreshortened and naturalistic; the figures depicted were actually distinguished residents of the city. Indeed, some of the models were WPA administrators who may not have realized how these renderings – of people enjoying good times, playing tennis, and riding horseback; and of women sometimes looking bored and desultory – would suggest the inequality and moodiness of the times.

In the center of the lobby you'll find a wonderful scale model diorama of Golden Gate Park.

Address 1000 Great Highway, San Francisco, CA 94121, +1 415.355.9400, www.beachchalet.com | Getting there Light rail: N-Judah (Judah St & La Playa Ave stop) | Hours Daily 8am–11pm | Tip An archery field lies just northeast of the Park Chalet. Lessons and equipment are available at the nearby San Francisco Archery Shop at 3795 Balboa Street.

13__The Beat Museum

Still on the road

William Burroughs's 1959 novel, *Naked Lunch*, begins: "I can feel the heat closing in, feel them out there making their moves, setting up their devil doll stool pigeons, crooning over my spoon and dropper … " This opening line taps into all the major themes of the Beats: paranoia, corrupt authority, addictions of every kind; and beneath the fear, the desire for new art forms, a new Romanticism, and a raw sound never heard before – a "howl," as Allen Ginsburg's signature poem describes it.

In 1948, Jack Kerouac proclaimed the "beat generation," with all the cultural meanings of that word: a beat to music; a beating from a nightstick. The origin of the Beats was the Upper West Side of Manhattan, but they spread to San Francisco and the Northwest, and so began the era that established the city's countercultural identity and created such iconic places as City Lights Books, where Lawrence Ferlinghetti still appears for readings. Most other places are gone, including Six Gallery on Fillmore Street, an underground exhibition space where Ginsburg first read "Howl," appearing along with five other great poets of the time.

The vibrations of the Beats can still be felt in an odd little museum located in the back of a bookstore on Broadway, half a block from City Lights, across the alley from the Hungry i strip club. Downstairs you'll notice Neal Cassady's 1949 Hudson covered in 5,000 miles of dust, prominently displayed among artwork, news articles, and various artifacts. The Hudson was donated to the Beat Museum by Walter Salles. It is not the original car but a prop used in the shooting of the movie *On The Road*. In the two small rooms upstairs are pieces of period furniture and signed first-edition books by Kerouac and others. The museum features readings, film viewings, and a two-hour guided walking tour that winds through North Beach exploring the places where these iconic writers lived and loved.

Address 540 Broadway Street, San Francisco, CA 94155, +1 415.399.9626, www.kerouac.com | **Getting there** Bus: 8X (Columbus Ave & Broadway St stop); 12 (Pacific Ave & Grant Ave stop); 30 (Stockton St & Columbus Ave stop) | **Hours** Thu–Mon 10am–7pm | **Tip** Just down the street on Adler Place is one of the city's great dive bars, Spec's – a living remnant of the beatnik era.

14 The Beehive

Retro forward

Valencia Street is one of the oldest yet trendiest neighborhoods in the city. Well known for being on the city's eclectic side, the area has also been known for one thing in particular: its women.

In the 70s, Valencia became known as a place "where the women are," and places like The Women's Building, the first women-led community center, were established. It was also the go-to place for the city's Lesbian community. Bars like Artemis Society, Amelia's, and even a bookstore called Old Wives' Tales thrived throughout the 80s. Many of these organizations and businesses no longer exist. Now, businesses like Good Vibrations and Osento serve as new attractions for the women of today.

Speaking of women, do you remember that popular hairstyle from the 60s called the 'beehive'? Well, of course, Valencia has a bar that's called The Beehive, a curated place that not only serves drinks, but also takes you back 50 years to when hair was big and style was funky. This bar captures that particular 'retro' mood that suggests the synthesis of nostalgia and jet-set cool, plus vague dissatisfaction with the present. Rebellious, blue-eyed, and ever iconic Steve McQueen would fit right in.

A glammed up, lounge-style bar with just the right amount of retro chic, features handcrafted cocktails and finger-licking eats, like fondue and meatballs. The ambiance exudes the 60s with its silk-screened mirrors, warm wood paneling, brass accents, low-slung couches, and geometric shapes of the honeycomb all around, combining the sweetness of honey with the dizziness of the 60s aesthetic. It is the perfect destination for nostalgia seekers, queen bees, wannabes, creators, and makers, and, like the rest of Valencia, just about anyone else! Be sure to try their signature eponymous drink, "The Beehive." Its sweet honey and dry gin make your flash back to the 60s just that much more fun.

Address 842 Valencia Street, San Francisco, CA 94110, www.thebeehivesf.com, info@thebeehivesf.com | Getting there BART to Daly City & Millbrae (16th St stop) | Hours Mon–Thu 5pm–midnight, Fri & Sat 2pm–2am, Sun 2–10pm | Tip For a stunning view of the city, walk 5 min west to Dolores Park.

15 Billionaires' Row

Life on the Gold Coast

The city's most famously expensive neighborhood is Pacific Heights, a district that's perhaps as much a state of mind as a financial statement. It's also known as the Gold Coast: before 1900 it was habitat for the demi-monde but afterward became an even wealthier enclave. These days it's a largely self-sufficient neighborhood with many of the city's best private schools, two splendid parks, and wish-upon-a-star homes that sell for upwards of $30 million.

Take a stroll along the stretch of Broadway between Buchanan and Lyon Streets, known as Billionaire's Row. The collection of houses – where every intricate, finely wrought decoration is executed to the last detail, from the paneling of the copper garage doors to the ornate brackets and window treatments – remind you of museum pieces. Indeed, these buildings are works of art. The stunning views are no small addition to the glory of the homes. Residents include old money and new, like philanthropists Ann and Gordon Getty and Apple's Sir Jonathan Ive.

The houses are architecturally diverse, from Gothic to Medi-terranean-style, Queen Anne to Dutch Revival, each one with a defining aesthetic: one a solid redbrick, another a limestone-colored extravagance of Corinthian columns or a minimalist mélange of glass and stucco. The common characteristic is grandeur, and perhaps the grandest of them all is the Spreckels Mansion at 2080 Washington Street, which was built in 1913 by a sugar baron; or the 11,000-square-foot Flood Mansion, at 2222 Broadway, whose luxurious interior rooms are available to rent for private events. The Victorian at 2640 Steiner Street is well known as a location in the movie *Mrs. Doubtfire*, starring the late Robin Williams.

Walking tours of the neighborhood begin regularly from the Haas-Lilienthal House on Franklin Street. It's the only house from the late 19th century open to the public.

Address Broadway Street between Divisadero Street & Lyon Street, San Francisco, CA 94115 | **Getting there** Bus: 22 (Fillmore St & Broadway St stop) | **Tip** Enjoy the cafes, restaurants, and boutiques on nearby vibrant and charming Fillmore Street, between Bush Street and Jackson Street.

16 The Bohemian Club

A private place for powerful men

The city is thick with elite men's clubs, but the most secretive, and lore-filled, is the Bohemian Club. The club was founded in 1872 and opened as a private saloon for journalists, then known as bohemians. Most worked in the newsroom at the Hearst-owned newspaper, the *San Francisco Examiner*. William Randolph Hearst was himself a member, as was poet Ambrose Bierce, who in 1901 wrote a poem, published in "The Ex," predicting the assassination of President McKinley. Not long afterward, an anarchist did exactly that. There was hell to pay in the club and the Hearst reporters left under a cloud to start another exclusive association called The Family. It still exists.

The Bohemian Club was always linked with artists, particularly musicians, but gradually became a fraternity for patricians from the private and public sector. Oscar Wilde, visiting the club in 1882, said, "I never saw so many well-dressed, well-fed, business-looking bohemians in my life."

Current and past members include Henry Kissinger, Colin Powell, Donald Rumsfeld, George Bush Sr. and Jr., Robert F. Kennedy, and Ronald Reagan – whose run for the presidency was decided at the Bohemian Club. Other club ventures include conceiving the Manhattan Project and mapping out the UN. Applicants often wait 15 years for an opening, as the club limits itself to about 2,700 members.

In recent years, the club has become like fine whiskey for conspiracy theorists obsessed by the "illuminati's" predilections, not the least of which is the club's annual retreat in Monte Rio, California, which is famously shrouded in mystery.

At the club's entrance in San Francisco there's the Bohemian mascot, an owl, symbolizing knowledge, and a plaque with this Shakespearean line, which is also the club's motto: "Weaving spiders come not here" – an elegant reminder to members not to do business in the clubhouse.

Address 624 Taylor Street, San Francisco, CA 94102 | **Getting there** Bus: 2, 3 (Post St & Taylor St stop) | **Hours** Members only | **Tip** A short walk uphill brings you to the Mark Hopkins and Fairmont Hotel.

17 Bourbon & Branch

The password-protected speakeasy

Naturally, San Francisco has its pretensions. In the Barbary Coast days, it was the city of "anything goes." In the sixties and seventies, it was "summer-of-love" central. In the eighties and nineties, it was all about the Rainbow Coalition. In the last 15 years, it's gone from hippies to hipsters. Most recently, the city has taken on the persona of an incubator for creative types of all kinds, from app designers to spoken-word artists.

If you're a visitor, it's sometimes difficult to distinguish affectation from authenticity. And, most of the time, the two are nearly inseparable. But that's part of what makes San Francisco so fun. Here's an example: in the upper Tenderloin, close to the theater district, next to an Indian restaurant on the corner of Jones and O'Farrell, a second-story sign above two nondescript storefronts reads, "Anti-Saloon League." And beneath that: "San Francisco Branch." This is Bourbon & Branch, a trendy bar modeled after a prohibition-era speakeasy that operated at this address in the 1920s. You make an online reservation, receive a password, show up, knock, and say the magic word. The door opens to a dimly lit bar, featuring handcrafted cocktails. There's also a speakeasy within the speakeasy called Wilson & Wilson (more strong drinks, different ambiance). When it's time to depart, you slip out a back door.

For those in search of an even more immersive and underground experience, there's The Speakeasy, an interactive theater event that transports you back to the 1920s. Details of each "happening" are kept under wraps until the day of, when guests are texted the location and password for entry. The audience is advised to dress in period clothes, ladies in their vintage flapper dresses and feathers, and gentlemen in their bowler hats with poker chips in their pockets. They mingle with the actors, and you can hardly tell the performers apart from the spectators.

Address 501 Jones Street, San Francisco, CA 94102, +1 415.346.1735, www.bourbonandbranch.com | Getting there Bus: 27 (Ellis St & Jones St stop); 38 (O'Farrell St & Leavenworth St stop) | Hours Daily 6pm–2am (reservation & password required) | Tip Don't have a B&B password? Enjoy a cocktail at the Redford, located at 673 Geary Boulevard, instead.

18 Buena Vista Park

A magical hush

It's been said that Buena Vista Park is the city's best outdoor makeout ballroom. Certainly the views of downtown and the Golden Gate Bridge are fetching, although less dramatic than from Corona Heights Park, which is higher up and just to the south. But Corona Heights Park is relatively bare, and in a cold wind, downright forbidding. Buena Vista, by comparison, is dense and – in the summer fog – mysterious and gothic. The trails switch back and forth up a slope, past nooks in the blackberry bushes, up old steps, and through a pine forest and one of the city's last oak groves. It offers a "magical hush" to the city, as one visitor put it.

Buena Vista is right in the middle of San Francisco, surrounded by Victorians and usually entered on the northern border that runs along Haight Street. It's the city's oldest park and is a favorite with dog walkers. It also features a tennis court, albeit in disrepair, and a small play area for children. Among the park's feathered inhabitants are several species that live in the Oak woodlands, including sapsuckers, brown creepers, and nuthatches.

The grounds also hold a cultural resonance. The drainage ditches that run here and there include fragments of unclaimed headstones from the cemeteries that were removed in the early twentieth century. The dead were reburied in Colma, and the recycled stone has been used in various city projects, including this one.

A word of caution: police have made a concerted effort to patrol the area, but that hasn't stopped all sorts of people from using the park – for all sorts of purposes. In other words, it's best not to visit at night.

However, there's a terrific day hike to be had that leads through Buena Vista Park up to Corona Heights Park and then down the other side of the hill into the Castro District using the Vulcan Steps, which are worth seeing in their own right.

Address Buena Vista Avenue & Haight Street, San Francisco, CA 94117, www.sfrecpark.org/destination/buena-vista-park | **Getting there** Bus: 6, 71 (Haight St & Buena Vista East or West Ave stop) | **Tip** Hitchcock fans will appreciate the building at 355 Buena Vista East Street, which appears in the classic thriller, *Vertigo*.

19_Building One

A sinking treasure

Treasure Island is that 400-acre heptagonal bit of landfill in the middle of San Francisco Bay, which is tethered to Yerba Buena Island – the midway anchor of the Oakland Bay bridge – by a causeway.

Treasure Island was built for the 1939 Golden Gate International Exposition – one of the grandest world fairs in West Coast history and dominated by an 81-foot-tall sculpture of a goddess known as *Pacifica*, created by San Francisco's foremost muralist and sculptor at the time, Ralph Stackpole. But just two years later, with war on America's doorstop, the fabulous "walled city" was demolished and the island was recast as a naval air station. Today, Treasure Island is a windy, moody offshoot of the city. It's also an affordable housing suburb with more than 2,000 residents. You'd think this must offer a terrific development opportunity, but the island is sinking, and at its northeastern end, the navy left the remains of an atomic warfare-training academy that used radioactive elements. The site closed in the 1990s but has yet to be cleaned up.

Still, the island has its attractions, including the great white administration building known as Building One. Constructed in 1938, it is a marvelous modern/deco-style relic from the exposition and you'll note the odd traffic-control tower on the roof, which was actually once functional. The architects were William Day and George Kelham. Day is known for several hotels in San Francisco, including the Mark Hopkins, and Kelham designed the city's old main library, now the Asian Art Museum. In 1989, the building stood in for the Berlin Airport in Steven Spielberg's *Indiana Jones and the Last Crusade.* In front of Building One there are half a dozen cast-stone statues representing different Pacific cultures. Inside, in the lobby, is a modest museum and notable murals. Behind the building you'll find a marina and wineries that offer tastings on the weekend.

Address Treasure Island Administration Building, Avenue of the Palms, San Francisco, CA 94130, +1 415.413.8462, www.treasureislandmuseum.org | Getting there Bus: 108 (Treasure Island Rd Guard Station stop) | Hours Mon–Fri 8:30am–5pm | Tip On the weekends, experience the flea market and wine tasting on Avenue of the Palms from 11am to 4pm.

20__Casa Cielo

"Sunny Jim" Rolph's love nest

Should you ever find yourself in Noe Valley, you'll notice many pretty, long-standing Victorians, which were built in rows in the early 20th century for working-class residents. The charm of the homes, along with the fact that the area has one of the best microclimates in San Francisco, attracts mostly families with kids, dogs, and strollers. The neighborhood to this day offers a sleepy feeling of remoteness from the city.

On the top of Liberty Hill, which is a short, steep walk from Dolores Park, you'll find magnificent views, from the Golden Gate Bridge to City Hall, the Bay Bridge and beyond. There, on the northeast corner of Sanchez and 21st Streets, you'll notice an imposing Tudor Revival house. Just inside the wrought-iron gates, under the shade of a pine tree, is a bronze statue of a lithe nymph balancing on a pedestal, surrounded by three graces.

The house, known as Casa Cielo, was built in 1931, and according to real-estate legend, was the occasional residence of then California governor "Sunny Jim" Rolph and his young mistress, Anita Page, the popular silent-film ingénue. As one story goes, the statue was a gift from Italian dictator Benito Mussolini to Page, who in turn gave it to Rolph.

According to a 2009 Historic Resource Evaluation Report, the truth is that "Sunny Jim" bought the lot vacant in 1927 and then sold it six weeks later to his son, who in turn sold it to a corporation in Burlingame in which his father had an interest. The house was built and Rolph's son lived in it briefly. Eventually, a prominent eye surgeon bought the property. Apparently, he had performed surgery on a relative of Mussolini, who gave him the statue as a gift. It's highly unlikely, therefore, that "Sunny Jim" ever lived in the house, much less Anita Page. That she was even ever Rolph's mistress is questionable. Apparently, however, the starlet did meet Mussolini.

Address Sanchez Street & 21st Street, San Francisco, CA 94114 | Getting there Light rail: J-Church (22nd St & Church St stop); Bus: 33 (18th St & Sanchez St stop) | Tip You'll find a great stair-climbing spot just one block south on 22nd Street between Church and Sanchez Streets.

21 Chinese Telephone Exchange

1500 names on the tip of the tongue

The early history of San Francisco's Chinatown is bleak, and the sordid details are often forgotten. It was the Chinese, who, in the mid-1800s, mined gold in the Sierra and built the Transcontinental Railroad. But by the late 1800s a national recession had stirred up public resentment toward cheap labor from abroad. In addition, the press's menacing portrayal of gambling, violence, opium dens, and prostitutes within the Chinese immigrant community gave lawmakers the opportunity to indulge in unabashedly racist policy making.

In those years, Chinatown was six blocks long, a tumultuous neighborhood roiling in gang wars. In about 1887, the community's first telephone service began and the Chinese Telephone Exchange opened in 1901 in a 3-tier pagoda on Washington Street, which was once home to the city's first newspaper, the *California Star*. You can still visit the building, now situated like a book on a crowded shelf, sandwiched between a noodle house and a souvenir shop.

In the beginning, the telephone exchange's manager brought in only male switchboard operators but gradually sought to hire women, who seemed to have a better disposition for such frenetic work. When the 1906 earthquake destroyed much of Chinatown, the exchange shut down for reconstruction. It was re-opened in 1909, after which only female operators were employed. They numbered about three-dozen, sitting in white tunics, earrings dangling, as they quickly plugged and unplugged lines on the board in front of them. Working hour after hour, they faced the daunting challenge of remembering the names of some 1500 subscribers. In addition, they had to be able to speak five local Chinese dialects, as well as English, and answer more than 13,000 calls a day. The exchange closed in 1949, with the coming of direct-dial rotary phones.

Address 743 Washington Street, San Francisco, CA 94108 | Getting there Bus: 1 (Clay St & Grand Ave stop); 30, 45 (Stockton St & Washington St stop) | Tip Stop at the Portsmouth Square Plaza to observe the Chinese chess or checkers games being played at the many tables there.

22 Clarion Alley

These walls can talk

The history of wall art in San Francisco begins with Diego Rivera, who is best remembered for his murals – and the political messages they contained. Some of his greatest works can be seen at City College, the San Francisco Art Institute (see ch. 96), and the Pacific Stock Exchange. He also influenced the murals found throughout the Mission District.

To see Rivera's legacy – now in the hands of a new generation of artists who may have never even heard his name – you need go to Clarion Alley. Located between 17th and 18th Streets, the alleyway connects Mission and Valencia Streets, two significantly different environments. Mission is filled with reminders of the longtime Latino community, who were the primary residents of the neighborhood until the late-nineties tech boom. Meanwhile, Valencia is the picture of order, with high-end shoppers and vested hipsters.

The alley itself is narrow and runs about 150 yards. The murals are naturally of mixed quality, and unfortunately some of the best work has been tagged, but if nothing else, this dazzling exhibit offers an organic history of the city. For instance, there are murals honoring the Black Panther movement and the Compton's Cafeteria riots in 1966, the first recorded incident of "militant queer resistance" in US history. The newest artworks reflect ongoing unrest between the city's working class and Silicon Valley's commuting class. "Bomb Condos Not Murals" and "Tax The Rich" are more recent themes in response to the changes in the neighborhood. Among the "message" murals is one by Mike Reger and Erin Amalia Ruch, titled *Narcania vs. Death*. It's a comic-book depiction of a young "heroine" struggling with heroin addiction who is saved from an opiate overdose by being given Narcan, or Naloxone. In the last panel, her concluding revelation is: "I don't know if there's anything worth living for but at least now I'll get the chance to find out."

Address Clarion Alley, San Francisco, CA 94110 | Getting there Bus: 22 (16th St & Valencia St stop); 33 (18th St & Valencia St stop); 49 (Mission St & 18th St stop) | Tip If you like innovative spicy Asian-inspired dishes, try the acclaimed Mission Chinese Food at 2234 Mission Street just around the corner – but be prepared to wait on line!

23 The Cloud Forest

Communing with nature on Mount Sutro

There are many sites with "Sutro" in their names all over the city. For example, there's the Sutro Baths at Lands End – the relics of a once spectacular indoor swimming pool, the largest in the world of the late 19th century. Across the street, up the hill, on the promontory above the Cliff House, there is Sutro Heights Park, where Adolph Sutro, a gold mining engineer, built his mansion to overlook his baths and the ocean. Now, all that's left of the magnificent structure is a pair of stone lions and a statue of Venus. And then there's the "cloud forest" on Mount Sutro, which offers one of the most sensuous and interesting less-traveled paths in the city.

Mount Sutro is an 834-foot-high hill, which, incidentally, supports a 977-foot three-legged steel tower – the Sutro Tower, which is the city's center pole, literally and figuratively. It transmits all of San Francisco's essential communications signals, including radio, television, wireless, and mobile. But of all the city's "Sutros," perhaps the most magical is to the north, in the Mount Sutro Open Space Preserve, which includes the 100-year-old Mount Sutro Forest. It consists of 80 acres dotted with eucalyptus trees, some of which stand 200 feet tall. It's a bird watcher's paradise, with 46 known species, including such characters as the great horned owl, the Pacific slope flycatcher, and the lime-yellow western tanager.

Several hiking trails wind through the woodland – not terribly long paths but satisfying ones, which are accessible from both Stanyan Street and Edgewood Avenue. The forest is a favorite respite from the arid nature of the city in these drought-full years. On those afternoons when the fog rolls in, the vegetation seems particularly lush and scented.

Often people flock to this geographical center of the city to get lost for a few hours, practice a walking meditation, or just to enjoy the lovely tree canopy overhead.

Address Mount Sutro, San Francisco, CA 94131, www.mntsutro.com | Getting there Bus: 6 (Parnassus Ave & Stanyan St stop) 43 (1697 7th Ave stop) | Tip At the East entrance to the forest is Cole Valley, with its many delightful cafes and small stores. Most of the businesses are still of the mom-and-pop variety. Stop for brunch at Zazie, a beloved local haunt, at 941 Cole Street.

24 The Condor Club

Death by piano

Once upon a time San Francisco was known for its vices, for its streetcars named desire, as it were. Now, not so much. The center of sensation, and relentless irreverence, has always been in North Beach along Broadway, with its string of nudie houses, sex shops, and Beat nightclubs like the Hungry i (*i* for *intellectual*or *id*, depending on which urban legend you believe). Bill Cosby started there; Lenny Bruce and Mort Sahl were regulars. These days, gentrification has led to fewer but more upscale strip clubs; including Showgirls and Larry Flynt's Hustler Club. Meanwhile, the iconic Hungry i is now the Hungry I Club, a down market strip joint a few doors from the original establishment.

The greatest of all the strip clubs on Broadway was the Condor, on the corner of Columbus. It's still there, with its vintage French quarter décor. In 1964, it became the first topless club in America; then the first bottomless club, in 1969. Carol Doda (born 1937), who studied at the San Francisco Art Institute, was the star of the show and, following 44 silicon injections, her breasts would be forever known as "the new twin peaks of San Francisco." She performed through the 1980s and her act always began with a piano being lowered from above and ended with her stripping down to a "monokini."

The Condor, which today combines strippers and sports, is known for a bizarre incident in 1983 when, one night after closing, a club bouncer got heavily involved with his girlfriend on top of the famous piano, which accidently began ascending, eventually pressing the couple against the ceiling. The bouncer died of asphyxiation while his girlfriend lay pinned underneath him. At 7am the next morning a janitor came upon the scene. It took emergency crews three hours to set the woman free. The white piano still hangs over the stage.

It's said that this gentlemen's club is also home to a secret bar in the back.

Address 560 Broadway Street, San Francisco, CA 94133, +1 415.781.8222, www.condorsf.com | **Getting there** Bus: 8X (Columbus Ave & Broadway St stop); 12 (Pacific Ave & Grant Ave stop); 30 (Stockton St & Columbus Ave stop) | **Hours** Daily 6pm–2am | **Tip** The historic Vesuvio cafe is just a block away at 255 Columbus Avenue. The bar was frequented by many Beat Generation personalities, including Jack Kerouac, Bob Dylan, Dylan Thomas, and Francis Ford Coppola.

25 Conservatory of Flowers

Home to the beautiful and the bizarre

James Lick was brilliantly weird, and a quintessential character in 19th-century San Francisco. He started out as the son of a carpenter in Pennsylvania, and wound up in Argentina in the 1820s crafting high-quality pianos. At one point he traveled to Europe and on his return voyage was captured by Portuguese mariners. He escaped, and eventually made his way to California, where he arrived just in time to catch the wave of the Gold Rush.

His genius was buying land, which he parlayed into hotels, farms, and other developments. Then, having become the richest man in the state, he set out to build huge statues of himself and his parents in downtown San Francisco. But just in the nick of time, the head of the Academy of Sciences rescued Lick from his delusions and directed his fortunes to other local projects, including a state-of-the-art observatory on Mount Hamilton east of San Jose, and also the Conservatory of Flowers, which is a replica of the Palm House in London's Kew Gardens.

The all white, wood and glass Victorian greenhouse for exotic plants is situated in Golden Gate Park, across from the tennis courts. Lick died before it was built, and for years the various pieces lay about in crates. The building finally opened in 1879, and though it escaped the 1906 earthquake unharmed, it subsequently burned down and was rebuilt, twice. In 1995, it was devastated once again by a winter storm and wasn't reopened until 2003.

There are three rooms in the conservatory: one with an assortment of orchids and vines; the others with lowland and highland tropics and aquatic plants. It's all a trove of the beautiful and bizarre. Note especially the carnivorous fanged pitcher plant from Borneo, known for its curious relationship with ants: the plant provides the ants with food and shelter in exchange for nutrients supplied by the little bugs.

Address 100 John F. Kennedy Drive, San Francisco, CA 94118, +1 415.831.2090, www.conservatoryofflowers.org | Getting there Bus: 5 (Fulton St & Arquello Blvd stop) | Hours Tues–Sun 10am–4:30pm | Tip At Martin Luther King Jr. Drive and Middle Drive East is the Garden of Shakespeare's Flowers, featuring plants and flowers mentioned in the Bard's poems and plays. You can try to guess the "name of the work" as you pass each of the 150-odd specimens.

26__Cow Palace

From moo to Who

In 1915, San Francisco was in many ways still a cow town. The livestock exhibit at the Pan Pacific International Exposition that year was so popular that the city fathers imagined a permanent home to host livestock trade shows. The initial idea was to build it in the Marina District, but that was eventually scrapped during the Great Depression, when critics questioned using public money to fund such a venture. One of the local editorial boards asked, "Why, when people are starving, should money be spent on a 'palace for cows'?" And thus the name: Cow Palace.

As it turned out the huge building became a WPA project that brought in thousands of laborers. In 1941, the Cow Palace was completed, not in the Marina, but out on Geneva Avenue, along the southern edge of the city in that area known as Crocker-Amazon. It has a steel-and-concrete roof that covers six acres. During World War II, it was used as a staging site for troops heading to the Pacific campaign.

With seating for as many as 16,500, after the war, the building became a popular venue for basketball games, ice shows, livestock and boat shows, roller derbies, the U.S. Heavyweight Boxing Championship, and the Ringling Bros. and Barnum & Bailey Circus. The Beatles kicked off their first North American tour at the Palace and all the great groups of the era performed there, including Prince, Nirvana, and the Who – in that extraordinary 1973 concert when drummer Keith Moon passed out from too many horse tranquilizers and was replaced by a fan in the audience.

These days the Cow Palace features not only its regular tenants such as the circus and the Golden Gate Kennel Club Dog Show, but also the popular annual Body Art Expo, where many visitors leave with a permanent souvenir tattooed on their skin or an extra piercing purchased from one of the 300 on-site tattoo and piercing artists.

Address 2600 Geneva Avenue, Daly City, CA 94014, +1 415.404.4100, www.cowpalace.com | **Getting there** Bus: 8X, 9 (Santos St & Geneva Ave stop) | **Tip** Take the Philosopher's Way trail above the Cow Palace and you'll enjoy vast swaths of untouched open space. Start at the parking lot southwest of the intersection of Mansell Street and Visitation Avenue.

27 Creativity Explored

Art for all

San Francisco's history is filled with progressive struggles and protests, for example, the 25-day occupation of a federal building in 1977 in support of disabled rights legislation that helped lay the groundwork for the passage of the Americans with Disabilities Act thirteen years later. It's all part of a growing sensitivity, which you also find occurring in the arts.

In recent years, the Paul K. Longmore Institute on Disability at San Francisco State University, along with the San Francisco Lighthouse for the Blind, has sponsored Superfest, the longest running disability festival in the world.

And then there is Creativity Explored, "where art changes life." With a small gallery in front and a large studio facility in the back, Creativity Explored is a nonprofit designed to support artists with developmental disabilities in the creation, exhibition, and sale of their work. Located in the Mission District, it is one of the city's many off-the-beaten-track treasures.

Creativity Explored was founded by Florence Ludins-Katz and Elias Katz in 1983, and provides various resources, including classes taught by professional artists, which afford attendees an opportunity to experiment with a variety of media and learn new techniques. Workshops offer instruction in figure drawing and painting, but also in wearable art, as well as printing techniques, papier-mâché, mapmaking, and "found-object sculpture." Those participating in the center's programs need not have any prior art-making experience, merely an interest in trying.

The works produced are often extraordinary. The exhibition openings at Creativity Explored are usually crowded and the gallery has become a vital part of the San Francisco art scene. Some of the artists' works have been included in international group shows, as well as museum exhibitions. The gallery is well worth a visit.

Address 3245 16th Street, San Francisco, CA 94103, +1 415.863.2108, www.creativityexplored.org | Getting there Bus: 22 (16th St & Guerrero St stop) | Hours See website for hours | Tip It's a short walk to the always-bustling Pizzeria Delfina (3611 18th Street) for chef/owner Craig Stoll's delicious super-thin and crispy pizza.

28 Crissy Field

From airfield to House of Air

Crissy Field forms a 130-acre puzzle piece of the city, stretching about a mile and a half from the St. Francis Yacht Club west along the bay to Fort Point, the forbidding Civil-War-era brick fortress underneath the San Francisco abutment of the Golden Gate Bridge (where Jimmy Stewart saved a suicidal Kim Novak in Hitchcock's *Vertigo*, though you can't visit the exact spot behind the fort because since 9/11 it's been gated off).

Originally an estuary, in 1919, Crissy Field became part of the Presidio and was made over into an army airfield, built largely on landfill as well as quite hazardous materials. It got its name from Major Dana H. Crissy, who was killed that year while flying in "a transcontinental reliability and endurance test." In 1994, the National Park Service took over the field and the man-made was unmade. Today, the field is literally a grand expanse of grass next to an estuary that's now home to such "flying machines" as the great egret, the great blue heron, the Caspian tern, and the brown pelican. The aircraft hangars have been converted to private enterprises, including a trampoline park called House of Air and a rock-climbing establishment.

The field is known primarily for its views of the bridge and walking trails, and for the windsurfers who use the shoreline as a jumping-off point to sail across the narrows. It's also been a showplace for large outdoor sculptures. In October 2013, Lisa Bielawa, a musician and arts impresario, orchestrated a 60-minute happening on the field that involved 800 musicians. This was a duplication of a similar event she presented at the former Tempelhof Airport outside Berlin. The musicians were organized into groups that gradually moved away from the center, each playing its own "melodic-orchestral signature": not unlike something the artist Christo would do, but with music. As Bielawa put it, "it's what he might call a 'gentle disturbance.'"

Address 603 Mason Street, San Francisco, CA 94129, www.parksconservancy.org/programs/crissy-field-center | **Getting there** Bus: 30 (Divisadero St & Chestnut St stop); 30X (Beach St & Divisadero St stop) | **Tip** Take a walk to the delightful Warming Hut on the west side of Crissy Field for a cozy drink or a snack on a chilly day.

29 Dashiell Hammett's Apartment

Where the Maltese Falcon took flight

One of the great masters of noire was Dashiell Hammett (1894–1961), who lived a few blocks west of Union Square in a fourth-floor apartment above a coin laundry. He resided there from 1926 to 1929, during which time he wrote his signature detective novels *Red Harvest, The Dain Curse*, and *The Maltese Falcon*. The last led to the film that launched the careers of director John Huston and actor Humphrey Bogart, who played the hollow-hearted dick, Sam Spade.

Hammett, a tall, thin man with white hair, black eyebrows, and a patrician look, is best remembered for crime fiction, but was also a fervent political activist. His affiliations with a Communist party front group led to a brief federal prison sentence in 1951. A few years later he was among the blacklisted of Hollywood. Then illness set in: he had contracted tuberculosis while serving in World War I (he also served in World War II), a condition made worse by years of relentless drinking and chain-smoking. It was his beloved friend, lover, and political comrade, playwright Lillian Hellman who, in those last years, brought him his dinner and a martini each night, and walked him up to death's door. She once called him a "Dostoyevsky sinner-saint."

The Post Street neighborhood that Hammett/Spade lived in was seedy back then. These days it's more blanche than noire. Hammett and his fictional hard-boiled private eye lived in Apt. 401, which is located on the northwest corner of the building and is revisited periodically in the local press. It's a small studio with a Murphy bed and a kitchen that's the size of a small rug. The current tenant has apparently carefully recreated Hammett's space.

To honor the 75th anniversary of *The Maltese Falcon's* publication, a wall plaque was placed on the side of the gated entrance. It reads simply: "Home of Dashiell Hammett and Sam Spade."

Address 891 Post Street, San Francisco, CA 94109 | Getting there Bus: 2, 3 (Post St & Hyde St stop) | Hours Viewable from the street only | Tip For a delicious Louisiana-style bread pudding, duck into Hooker's Sweet Treats at 442 Hyde Street.

30 David Ireland's House

Artist as hunter

The Mission District around 20th and Capp Streets is good place to alight. On Mission Street, Bruno's Nightclub used to be trendy for being upscale in an iffy neighborhood — you'd look up from your martini and suddenly you felt like you were in an episode of The Sopranos. Now, the neighborhood is much calmer and the vibe is hip. You feel it in various forms, not least on Capp Street at the Community Music Center, one of the true secrets of the Mission District. It's a music school with a small performance hall, which has become a popular concert venue for local musicians playing classical music, jazz, and tango.

Just a block down on the actual corner of Capp and 20th Street, there's a largely unknown venue in the local art world: David Ireland's house, now The 500 Capp Street Foundation.

Ireland (1930-2009) was a tall, lanky, silver-haired artist. To some, Ireland had the look of a 1950s movie star, and for a time he owned a "safari" store on Union Street. He was often seen sweeping his front porch of his house, acquired in 1975. The house was not just his home and his art studio; it was his evolving artwork. In this two-story Victorian, built in 1886, he striped down the walls, some rounded, to variations of yellow, glistering, raw surfaces. He gave lavish dinners for 14 at a long narrow table in a dining room marked by antelope skulls, hanging sculptures, and crude cement candleholders. The atmosphere suggested a salon for San Francisco artistic and intellectual minds. He used found objects. His work was gritty and urban, minimalist, and suggested a mockery of politesse. In one room, he used acetylene torches as light fixtures. He hung chairs on a rounded wall, and highlighted cracks and rotting window frames. The wood floors were paint splattered.

David lived to see his house purchased and preserved by the 500 Capp Street Foundation.

Address 500 Capp Street, San Francisco, CA 94110, +1 415.872.9240, www.500cappstreet.org | **Getting there** Bus 14R (20th St stop) | **Hours** Tours Wed–Sat 11 & 2pm | **Tip** For an evening city view and a drink, walk two blocks west to El Techo at 2516 Mission Street.

31 The F-Line

A journey back in time

While San Francisco's little cable cars are busy "climbing halfway to the stars" (as the classic Tony Bennett song goes) most residents rely on a bus and streetcar system known as MUNI. Though MUNI is comprehensive enough to make living in the city without a car a real option, it is also famous locally for running late or breaking down. One critic noted that MUNI is emblematic of the city's "Italian Complex," which is a nod to the contrast between the city's resplendent beauty and dysfunctional administrations.

But there is one light in the MUNI fog: the six-mile-long F-line, a heritage streetcar service created in 1995 to replace a much faster bus line. The old streetcars come from around the world, each with the name of its original city still in the window.

The F-line features a panorama of retro designs. For example, there's an Art Deco "torpedo," built in the 1950s, which looks like a two-tone Ferragamo shoe. And then there are the famous Peter Witt cars, in their bright orange livery. Witt, who was from Cleveland, was known for being "rebellious and outspoken," exactly the temperament of San Francisco. Witt's design was adopted by Italy and became popular in Milan in the 1920s. The design featured a layout with an exit in the middle of the car manned by a conductor; passengers could therefore enter in the front and pay either upon exiting or when they moved to a better seat in the rear.

The F serves both residents and tourists as it stretches along Market Street north from the Castro District through downtown, past the Tenderloin, the Palace Hotel, and all the way down to the Ferry Building, then west along the piers on the Embarcadero to Fisherman's Wharf.

The beauty and elegance of the streetcars evokes a time when the public and communal ritual of traveling through an American city was as much about the journey as the destination.

Address Inbound toward Fisherman's Wharf, Outbound toward Castro District, San Francisco, CA, www.sfmuni.com/F | Tip The fare is the standard $2.25; Clipper cards are accepted too.

32 Flora Grubb Gardens

Coffee and air plants, anyone?

Flora Grubb Gardens is located in an area that has been considered, until quite recently, the city's nether regions, but is now on the leading edge of gentrification. It's off the 3rd-Street corridor, down in the Bay View district, a neighborhood still better known for homicides than horticulture.

This 2,800-square-foot garden center includes an espresso bar and offers periodic lectures on topics such as green architecture, hanging gardens or innovative landscape design. The selection of available vegetation is broad. There are palm trees, Japanese maples, succulents, shrubs, and grasses, all set out in beautiful pots, or in unconventional holders, like hanging bicycles and an old Ford Edsel. There are also a variety of exquisite vertical gardens displayed throughout the center, which gives the space the feeling of a living art gallery. At the core of Flora Grubb is a deep interest in collaboration – this is a place where all kinds of artisans create their own synchronicities – and the results are a bit magical.

The small coffee counter is hosted by the coffee-roasting company Ritual Coffee and houses an espresso machine and a five-ring pour-over bar crafted from copper piping. You can enjoy your latte at the cafe tables or on the heated cast-stone sofa in the charming garden patio – you may never want to get up!

Flora Grubb is a woman with a deep affinity for gardens; she has nurtured this "rustic urban" oasis since opening in 2007. She once described her Earth Day wish in an interview with Grace Bonney: "It is always my wish that I'm helping people to create gardens that they love … and that the connection they make to nature through their garden will inspire them to live more gently on the planet. It is my wish that more and more people will turn to their gardens to find sanctuary, and that they will develop a love for growing things that will stay with them for their whole lives."

Address 1634 Jerrold Avenue, San Francisco, CA 94124, +1 415.626.7256, www.floragrubb.com | **Getting there** Bus: 23 (Jerrold Ave & Phelps St stop) | **Hours** Wed–Sun 11am–6pm | **Tip** *Nearby is Bayview Rise*, a big, bold, playful mural painted on the 187-foot shaft of a grain silo (Pier 92, off 3rd Street).

33 The Fly-Casting Pools

Angling for a good time

Among the anachronisms in Golden Gate Park are the two windmills at the park's western edge, which were built at the turn of the last century and pumped 70,000 gallons of water an hour in an effort to help root the park to its site on top of vast sand dunes. In 1913, electric pumps took over and the windmills fell to ruin. Restorations for both were completed between 1981 and 2012. This is a particularly beautiful and less traveled part of the park, which harbors many other pleasant surprises, including the small lakes and walking paths west of the Polo Fields. Among the glades, off a trail in the reeds, you'll also come upon an occasional "sacred space." The much-revered ecofeminist and neopagan activist Starhawk has held ceremonies in this area at the solstices.

Nearby, in a grove of eucalyptus trees behind the police stables, is one of the park's lesser-known and most curious features: a pair of fly-casting pools. They are located next to the clubhouse for the Golden Gate Angling and Casting Club, an international club that opened in 1933 and whose members include some of the greatest casters of all time. The ponds themselves are considered world class and have been the site for many competitions. Free casting lessons for all levels are available to nonmembers at various times throughout the year.

In 2000, Thomas McGuane, novelist, filmmaker, and one of the country's great sportswriters, wrote a description of the club's members in his essay *The Longest Silence: A Life in Fishing*: "The group is not quite heterogeneous, and though its members seem less inclined to dressing up than many of San Francisco's populace, they are not the Silent Majority's wall of flannel, either. To be exact, sartorially, there is no shortage of really thick white socks here, sleeveless V-neck sweaters, or brown oxfords. The impression, you suppose, is vaguely up-country."

Address McLaren Angler's Lodge and Fly Casting Pools, 1232 John F. Kennedy Drive, San Francisco, CA 94121, +1 650.270.7258, www.ggacc.org | Getting there Bus: 5 (Fulton St & 36th Ave stop) | Tip Rhododendron Island, at JFK Drive and 36th Avenue, is home to 400 rhododendrons, blooming once a year, with different varieties showing color between February and May.

34__Fog Bridge

A walk in the clouds at the Exploratorium

If there's one weather element that captures the zeitgeist of San Francisco, it's fog – in all its many forms. There's the unruly, roughneck fog that batters traffic crossing the Golden Gate Bridge, the desultory fog that lays about like the destitute on cold nights downtown, and the swarming wisps that blow through Golden Gate Park. Fog is the perfect metaphor for all the city's mysteries and ambiguities. Filmmakers of noir have always known that about San Francisco.

The conditions that bring fog into the city are unique to the region. It's a phenomenon that occurs particularly during the summer months, when the fog generally burns off by midday; hence you'll hear people refer to "May gray" and "June gloom." It's the 50-degree Pacific Ocean currents together with cold moist air out of Alaska that produce a vast cool air mass that collides with the warmer air onshore.

In homage to this aspect of San Francisco's identity is a permanent and free exhibit at the Exploratorium museum, which you'll find on Piers 15 and 17 along the Embarcadero. The outdoor installation *Fog Bridge #72494* by Japanese artist Nujiko Nakaya involves walking across a narrow 150-foot-long bridge connecting the two piers while, four times per day, 800 high-pressure nozzles emit bursts of swirling artificial fog. Being instantly blinded in the cloud of dense white mist is both disorienting and exhilarating.

Once you've come through the fog, a longer visit to the inside of the Exploratorium – which the *New York Times* called "the most important science museum to have opened since the mid 20th century" – is highly recommended. There are hundreds of constantly changing exhibits; nearly all have some interactive hands-on aspect to engage young minds and pique curiosity. One recent exhibit, an exploration of the "Science of Sharing," had museumgoers investigate themselves through social interaction, particularly in the areas of competition and cooperation.

Address Exploratorium, Pier 15, San Francisco, CA 94111, +1 415.528.4444, www.exploratorium.edu | **Getting there** Streetcar: F-Line (Embarcadero & Green St stop) | **Hours** Daily 10am, noon, 2pm & 4pm; Thu also 7pm | **Tip** Walk a couple blocks south to experience the ultimate San Francisco gourmet heaven at the Ferry Building Marketplace on the Embarcadero at Market Street.

35__Foreign Cinema

Dinner and a show

For years, the Mission District was regarded as a cultural and economic refuge from the rest of the city, a largely Spanish-speaking enclave noted for its taquerias, cheap rents, and annual Carnival festival. The Mission was also a relatively dangerous neighborhood, particularly around Garfield Square, at 26th and Harrison Streets; and along the Mission Street corridor from 16th to 24th Streets. In the mid-1990s, red and blue colors still signified the fiefdoms of the Nortenos and Surenos. Now the gangs have subsided, crime is less intense, and following the tech boom that began in the mid 2000s, gentrification has set in.

One sign of change is the number of new dance studios, work lofts, nonprofits, and ever-trendier restaurants looking to distinguish themselves in a city full of Michelin stars. One of the most adored restaurants is Foreign Cinema, which opened in 1999. The eatery has become a darling of San Francisco thanks to its eccentric but upscale combination of cuisine, art, and film. The seasonal and oft-changing California Mediterranean menu is orchestrated by the famous chef/owner duo of Gayle Pirie and John Clark.

Foreign Cinema's stylish interior is masked by a fifties-era theater-marquis-style exterior on a seedy stretch of sidewalk, a few doors down from the boarded-up New Mission Theater, which is poised for restoration and development. Inside, movies are projected on the cement wall of an al fresco courtyard – just one of the many defined spaces where one can dine or enjoy a cocktail.

The foreign, independent and classic films screened nightly include such noir favorites as *The Maltese Falcon* and Truffaut's *Day for Night*. An adjoining gallery space called Modernism West, overseen by acclaimed art dealer Martin Muller, has exhibited the crème de la crème of the art world, including the work of Mel Ramos and Mark Stock.

Address 2534 Mission Street, San Francisco, CA 94110, +1 415.648.7600, www.foreigncinema.com | **Getting there** Bus: 14, 49 (Mission St & 22nd St stop) | **Hours** Daily 5:30–11pm, Sat & Sun brunch 11am–2:30pm | **Tip** After dinner, dance the night away to African beats at the Little Baobab around the corner at 3388 19th Street.

36 Fort Funston

Where humans take to the sky

Ask longtime residents what makes San Francisco great, and often they'll tell you about the wild places along the coastal edges. Locals know the city is only a veneer; behind it, a tenuous outpost of civilization on a craggy peninsula, forever battered by wind and water. Nowhere is this wild aspect more tangible than at Fort Funston, atop 200-foot-high bluffs overlooking the Pacific across from the Olympic Club golf course. The fort was an army defense installation during World Wars I and II; during the Cold War, it was a Nike missile launch site. Now, trails scatter in every direction, winding down through dense trees, ice plants, coastal scrub, and tunneled fortifications once filled with artillery.

The bluffs have become one of California's premier departure points for hang gliders, popular year-round but especially in March and October, when the offshore breezes pick up. The hang-gliding launch spot is at the western edge of the parking lot. An observation deck with benches provides a great vantage point to observe giant-winged humans as they run off the cliff and take flight. Some afternoons a dozen or more gliders fill the sky, set out in a row above the bluffs as though in formation, or else carving slow-motion arcs between the blue of sea and sky.

A long stairway with cable railings leads down to the beach, where at low tide, visitors can walk in either direction for quite a distance. Bird enthusiasts will note the hundreds of nests built into the cliffside by Bank Swallows, once a common coastal species, now endangered. This is also a hugely popular place for horseback riders; and it is a dog walker's paradise, because it's one of the few places in the city where dogs can be off leash.

Be warned: the surf is treacherous, with powerful undertows. And keep in mind that the stairway is a long, strenuous climb – and if you go down, you must come up!

Address 206 Fort Funston Road, San Francisco, CA 94132, www.nps.gov/goga/planyourvisit/fortfunston.htm | Getting there Bus: 18 (John Muir Dr & Skyline Blvd stop) | Tip It's almost always gusty at Fort Funston, so a windbreaker is a must. For a stunning vista, stop at the wooden viewing platform just next to the parking lot.

37 The Frank Lloyd Wright Building

A mid-century jewel in the Barbary Coast

The world is filled with Maiden Lanes, each with their own contradictions. There's London's Maiden Lane, which runs by Covent Garden – a road originally known for the stink from the beasts of burden. Or Maiden Lane in Manhattan, once a lovers' path, and then the center of the jewelry district until the early 1900s. San Francisco's Maiden Lane, off Union Square, was first called Morton Street in the late 19th century, and was a main vein through the Barbary Coast. That was the city's rough and ready district, known for a murder a week and the bordellos run by that incomparable lord of the underworld, Jerome Bassity. He wore three gold rings on each hand and ran 200 ladies in his demimonde.

These days the only "maidens" strolling the lane are strictly members of the wealthy elite, ever sensitive to the seductive windows of Chanel, Yves Saint Laurent, and the like. They shop the boutiques and sit at the outdoor cafes, listening to the "Italian opera tenor of Maiden Lane," a portly man in suspenders named Robert Close.

In some guidebooks, Maiden Lane is listed as a two-block pedestrian mall, but this is not a scaled-down version of Rodeo Drive. Maiden Lane is straightforward, and European, and more charming and moody in that sense. It's also distinguished architecturally by the only Frank Lloyd Wright building in San Francisco, at Number 140, with its arched entryway in a facade of tan brick. The interior brings to mind the spiral walkway of the Solomon R. Guggenheim Museum in New York and some say that the building, erected in 1948, was the museum's prototype. The translucent globes suspended above the circular space illuminate the interior filled with curved rooms and ramps. Originally the V. C. Morris Gift Shop, it's now a home to the Xanadu Gallery of ethnographic art.

Address 140 Maiden Lane, San Francisco, CA 94108 +1.415.500-4930, www.isaia.it | **Getting there** Bus: 2, 3 (Post St & Grant Ave stop) | **Hours** By appointment only | **Tip** Around the corner is the 49 Geary building, housing four floors of art and photo galleries.

38 Gallery 6

The ghosts of Vertigo at the Legion of Honor

Alfred Hitchcock's *Vertigo*, which opened in 1958, was shot almost entirely in the city of San Francisco, and for fans of the "Master of Suspense," many locations remain accessible. The Empire Hotel, where Jimmy Stewart finds an ever-sultry Kim Novak, is still at 940 Sutter Street – now named the Hotel Vertigo. You can even book Room 501, where Novak's character Judy lived. The Podesta Baldocchi flower shop, visited by Novak's other character, Madeleine, also is still in business, although no longer at its original address.

And then there's the Legion of Honor museum. In the particularly haunting scene filmed there, Madeleine sits in Gallery 6 contemplating the *Portrait of Carlotta*, a life-sized painting of a woman she strongly resembles. Hitchcock took a week to get the lighting in the gallery just right. Incidentally, Gallery 6 holds the work of such French Baroque painters as Claude Lorrain, Georges de La Tour, Louis Le Nain, Eustache Le Sueur, and Simon Vouet, and recently added a painting by Laurent de La Hyre (1606–1656), *Allegory of Geometry*.

Portrait of Carlotta was created by American Abstract Expressionist painter John Ferren (1905–1970). Sadly, the painting was eventually lost. Ferren, who also painted Stewart's "nightmare sequence" in *Vertigo*, briefly went to art school in San Francisco and eventually made his way to Paris, where he was greatly influenced by Matisse and Kandinsky.

The Legion of Honor is a neoclassical building sitting on the top of a grassy cliff at Lands End, overlooking the Pacific Ocean with the Golden Gate Bridge and Marin Headlands to the north and the Lincoln Park Golf Course to the south. The building, constructed expressly as a gift to the city from Alma de Bretteville Spreckels, was completed in 1924. The Legion's timeless elegance was inspired by the Palais de la Légion d'Honneur in Paris, also known as the Hôtel de Salm.

Address Legion of Honor, 100 34th Avenue, San Francisco, CA 94121, +1 415.750.3600, www.legionofhonor.famsf.org | **Getting there** Bus: 18 (Legion of Honor stop) | **Hours** Tue–Sun, 9:30am–5:15pm | **Tip** At the edge of Lincoln Park, at California Street and 32nd Avenue, you'll find a stunning Art Nouveau-inspired bench and steps, recently restored and hand tiled by the artist Aileen Barr.

39 The Gardens of Alcatraz

Planting life on "the Rock"

Alcatraz Island, the top of an ancient hill peaking out of the San Francisco Bay, is located just a mile and a half off the Embarcadero. The legendary island houses the remains of a once formidable federal penitentiary – from which only three inmates, working together, may have successfully escaped. Evidence of their survival remains inconclusive to this day: a raft found on Angel Island, footprints leading away, unconfirmed sightings of the fugitives, postcards in the men's handwriting. The infamous breakout was in June 1962; the next year the prison closed down after 30 years in operation.

Anyone who imagines this might not have been such an agonizing incarceration need only pay a visit to Alcatraz and walk through some of the abandoned facilities – the main cellblock, the dining hall, the library, the hospital, the morgue – to sense the hopeless and isolating effect of the relentless fog, wind, and siren song of the city itself, so torturously close.

Beginning in 1861, when the government officially started using the existing military fortification on Alcatraz as a military prison, an effort was made to improve the island's aesthetic. In 1865, Victorian-style gardens began to bloom, and in the 1920s, prisoners planted hundreds of trees and shrubs, along with terraces and a rose garden.

Among those who contributed to the gardens was a counterfeiter named Elliott Michener who had tried unsuccessfully to escape from Leavenworth State Prison in 1941 and was subsequently sent to Alcatraz. He quickly won the trust of the guards after returning a dropped key. For nine years he took charge of the gardens and, in addition to ordering bulbs and seeds, built a greenhouse and toolshed. "If we are all our own jailers, and prisoners of our traits," he once wrote, "then I am grateful for my introduction to the spade and trowel, the seed and the spray can. They have given me a lasting interest in creativity."

Address Alcatraz, San Francisco, CA 94123, www.alcatrazgardens.org | **Getting there** Ferry leaves from Pier 33 on the Embarcadero; tickets are $30 | **Hours** 9am to the evening | **Tip** Dress in layers and wear comfortable shoes. You'll have to walk a good distance around the island and it gets cold and windy.

40_The GLBT Historical Society Museum

It was a long journey

San Francisco has long been a sanctuary for those seeking acceptance, providing a haven for individuals who have faced rejection elsewhere. The lesbian, gay, bisexual, transgender, and queer (LGBTQ) community found a true home in the Castro District, nestled just below Twin Peaks, between Market and 20th Streets. This area, once an Irish working-class neighborhood, was transformed in the 1960s, as the LGBTQ community began to unite and assert its presence. One of the most courageous leaders during this time was Harvey Milk, who owned a camera store in the Castro. His election to the city's Board of Supervisors in 1973 marked a significant milestone, which was further celebrated with the election of liberal state Senator George Moscone as mayor. Tragically, both Milk and Moscone were assassinated on November 27, 1978, in City Hall.

This dark moment was followed by one of the most challenging periods in San Francisco's history: the AIDS crisis of the 1980s, which brought unimaginable grief and loss to countless families and friends. In a powerful show of solidarity and resilience, the community organized the first Folsom Street Fair in 1984 – not just as a celebration, but as a significant act of visibility and defiance against the adversity they faced.

In 1985, the GLBT Historical Society was established. In 2011, they founded the GLBT Historical Society Museum as a testament to the struggles and triumphs of this vibrant community, ensuring that the voices and stories of the past are never forgotten.

The museum's permanent collection includes a segment of one of the original eight-color rainbow flags from 1978. The exhibition features photographs and artifacts that illustrate everyday queer life in San Francisco, showcasing artists from the LGBTQ community.

Address 4127 18th Street, San Francisco, CA 94114, +1 415.777.5455, www.glbthistory.org/museum | Getting there Take the K Balboa Metro to the Castro Metro Station, then walk to 18th Street | Hours Tue–Sun 11am–1pm, 1:30–5pm | Tip One of the most significant historic places on Castro is The Castro Camera and the Harvey Milk Residence, which is now a gallery and a gathering space, Queer AF (573 Castro Street, www.queerartsfeatured.com).

41 Glen Canyon Park

A time machine to the San Francisco of yore

Glen Canyon Park is an out-of-the-way park you won't find in traditional guidebooks. In fact, if you happen to ask a local about it, they're likely to say, "Oh yes, I forgot about that." And they may even add, "I wish everyone else did too."

Located in a neighborhood below Twin Peaks, the park's entrance leads to a recreation center that includes courts and playing fields. Beyond that, a seventy-acre "wilderness" begins: the ground rises, sometimes sharply; eucalyptus groves gradually trail off, and a series of paths wind along a creek through the scrub to the north. The canyon sides are steep – not dangerous, but steep. Rock climbers practice "bouldering" here. It's a pleasant walk, although some might consider it more of a gentle hike. Even for semi-serious runners, a jog here is demanding.

You can reach the trails at various points, including from the recreation center, although parking is sometimes difficult, particularly on Saturdays when small children run about for soccer practice. Otherwise, you can drive up to the Diamond Heights Shopping Center and work your way down into the canyon.

The park is a natural time machine: Unlike Golden Gate Park, Glen Park Canyon is raw and very much the way the city looked in the late nineteenth century. And there are regulations to keep it that way, including stringent leash laws for dogs. Which is good, if you're not a dog owner, because there's a healthy amount of wildlife to observe, including red-tailed hawks, great-horned owls, alligator lizards, and coyotes. You'll see many signs warning you of their presence and suggesting you make a lot of noise if the animals get within fifty feet. They rarely do. When you do see them, it's mostly in the early morning or evening. Inevitably it's an unexpected encounter, but once eye contact is made, you'll find they're quickly off to their next appointment.

Address Elk Street & Chenery Street, San Francisco, CA 94127, www.sfrecpark.org/venue/glen-canyon-park | Getting there Bus: 44 (O'Shaughnessy Blvd & Del Vale Ave stop) | Tip The Glen Park "village" around Cheney and Diamond Streets has a suburban vibe with some restaurants, a bar, a market, and a library.

42 Glide Memorial Church

Can I get an amen?

Lizzie Snyder, born in 1852 to a Methodist family in Louisiana, married a cattle baron in Sacramento named Joseph Glide and became an important figure in the local peace-and-justice movement of the day. When Joseph died in 1909, Lizzie inherited his business and became quite successful while continuing her charitable work. In 1914, she opened a safe house for women and then, in 1929, she bought land in downtown San Francisco and built the Glide Memorial United Methodist Church in the heart of the Tenderloin, on the corner of Ellis and Taylor Streets.

There are many houses of worship in San Francisco – it's a far more religious town than you might suspect, considering its image among the faint of heart as Sodom and Gomorrah. But of all the city's holy sites, Glide is the one place it seems that everyone who lives here, regardless of denomination, ethnicity, race, politics, or sexual orientation, has visited at some point, if only to hear the ensemble choir belting out joyful gospel music or the sermons of the church's charismatic minister and local hero, Cecil Williams.

Williams arrived on the scene in 1963, a young African American with conviction, courage, and a heart as big as the city he ministers to. He took in all the people who had nowhere to go: prostitutes, Black Panthers, resistors of every ilk, as well as estranged matrons in Pacific Heights. He is truly a beloved local character. Whether providing assistance in the fight against poverty, drugs, AIDS, or any other epidemic facing the community, Glide and its pastors have been the city's keel for many decades. They serve an average of 2,500 meals per day to those in need, which is evidenced by the frequent line of homeless and hungry people outside the church.

Simply put, when people talk about San Francisco being a progressive place, Reverend Williams and Glide Church are what they're talking about.

Address 330 Ellie Street, San Francisco, CA 94102, +1 415.674.6000, www.glide.org | **Getting there** Bus: 27 (Ellis St & Taylor St stop); 38 (O'Farrell St & Taylor St stop) | **Hours** Sunday service 9am & 11am | **Tip** Just three blocks north is The Warfield, the historic music venue, where you can hear some of the best musicians performing in an intimate Art Deco theatre.

43 Grace Cathedral Labyrinths

A maze for meditation

There are more than 70 publicly accessible labyrinths in the Greater Bay Area; 15 in San Francisco alone. You find them in schoolyards and courtyards, in naves and parks, even on a cliff. At Lands End, for example, above a hidden cove, there is a stone labyrinth that is particularly popular during equinoxes and solstices (see ch. 55). These labyrinths vary in design – from classical to Cretan, from 7 to 11 circuits, from 24 to 60 feet across – and they vary in materials, too. One is made of herbs, beans and flowers; another, from pack cloth and rope. Others are painted on concrete or wood. One is designed for the blind.

The most notable of all these are the two atop Nob Hill at Grace Cathedral, the Episcopal church that opened in 1964 and is distinguished by its French Gothic design. In 1991, the Reverend Dr. Lauren Artress, a priest long associated with the cathedral, went on sabbatical and, by accident or providence, discovered the mystery and power of labyrinths. Upon her return, she oversaw the precise reproduction of the medieval eleven-circuit labyrinth found at the cathedral at Chartres. The first rendering was on canvas, then in a tapestry, and in 1995, a terrazzo labyrinth was laid out in the Grace Cathedral Interfaith Meditation Garden. Two years later, a second labyrinth, made of limestone, was built into the floor in the nave.

Reverend Artress has been credited with restoring the labyrinth – as well as the practice of walking meditation – to the Christian tradition. There are three stages in the "feeling journey" through a labyrinth. The first is Purgation, or releasing, which is done on the way to the center. Once there, the ritual calls for Receiving, which consists of meditation or prayer. And then on the Return, one reaches out to one's higher power, whatever that might be. It can be a process of both spiritual insight and personal redemption.

Address 1100 California Street, San Francisco, CA 94108, +1 415.749.6300, www.gracecathhedral.org | Getting there Bus: 1 (Clay St & Mason St stop); 27 (Leavenworth St & California St stop) | Hours Daily 8am–6pm | Tip For a perfect Mai Tai, visit the Tonga Room and Hurricane Bar at 950 Mason Street, the Fairmont Hotel's tropical lounge and a local institution since 1945.

44 The Green Roof

The Academy of Sciences goes "underground"

Among the delicacies of Golden Gate Park is the Academy of Sciences, a research center in the areas of biodiversity and sustainability, and a natural history museum. Generations of the city's children have grown up visiting the Steinhart Aquarium, the Morrison Planetarium, and the beloved dioramas of California's natural wonders, featuring life-size figures of Ohlone Indian maidens paddling by in their boats made of Tule reeds, with stuffed egrets peeking out of the surrounding weeds.

When the Academy of Sciences was rebuilt in 2008, many of the lifelike tableaux disappeared and were replaced with actual living environments, including a tropical rain forest enclosed in a 90-foot-tall glass dome; a Philippine coral reef; and a 2.5-acre garden on the roof complete with several knolls and a tapestry of native flora chosen for their ability to thrive on little water, high winds, and salt spray from the ocean. The nine species of plants selected were started in bio trays made of coconut husks, which allowed their roots to entwine and so permit the plants to hold each other in place on slanting surfaces. This "living roof" helps cool the building and provides a sanctuary for birds and butterflies.

The transformation of the museum into a state-of-the-art "green building" was all the genius of the Italian architect Renzo Piano (b. 1937), who is best known in recent years for the Shard in London and the Nemo Science Center in Amsterdam. His idea for the Academy of Sciences was to "raise up the park, and put the museum under it." Besides the green roof, the building was constructed with recycled concrete and steel, bits of reused denim for insulation, an irrigation system that utilizes rainwater, and natural lighting in 90 percent of the occupied spaces. As the *New York Times* put it, the building is a "comforting reminder of the civilizing function of great art in a barbaric age."

Address California Academy of Sciences, 55 Music Concourse Drive, San Francisco, CA 94118, +1 415.379.8000, www.calacademy.org | **Getting there** Bus: 44 (Academy of Sciences stop) | **Hours** Mon – Sat 9:30am – 5pm, Sun 11am – 5pm | **Tip** Every Thursday evening you can explore the museum while sipping a cocktail or just listening to music, during NightLife at the Academy.

45 The Hallidie Building

Ahead of its time

Hidden in the recesses of downtown, one can find an urban San Francisco that turns away from the grandeur of the California landscape and embraces the architectural ethos of an older metropolis. Call it the city's New Yorkishness, or its Chicagoisms, but from the shadowed blocks below the skyscrapers, the angles of stone and glass evoke a different aesthetic. Commerce, profit, and above all, the glorious future, are expressed in this architecture. And just as Chicago had Louis Sullivan, San Francisco had Willis Polk. Polk left dozens of distinctive buildings in the city, but none as influential with regard to the look of American cities in the last 100 years as the Hallidie building.

When it was built in 1917, the building was one of the first in the world to use glass curtain-wall construction, wherein the exterior glass wall attached directly to the structural steel framework. This innovation became the basis for the modern skyscraper. Although small by current standards, the seven-story Hallidie Building shines like the gem that it is. The façade has been restored, along with the contrasting Gothic grillwork and balconies. The transparency of the design, intended to bring space and light into the workplace, is intensely obvious here, as one seems to be looking through a huge window into a vast interior world. Currently, the space quite appropriately houses the offices of the San Francisco chapter of the American Institute of Architects.

Named for the cable-car pioneer Andre Hallidie, the building is now privately owned, though it originally belonged to the University of California; the blue and gold of the steel trim are the school's colors. There's a US Post Office branch on the ground floor, so it's easy to step inside to get a feel for the interior. The best way to get an overall view, however, is from the upper levels of the Crocker Galleria directly across the street.

Address 130 Sutter Street, San Francisco, CA 94104 | Getting there Bus: 2 (Post St & Montgomery St stop); 3 (Sansome St & Sutter St stop); 30, 45 (Stockton St & Sutter St stop) | Tip Just a block away you'll find the Crown Zellerbach Building, at One Bush Plaza, San Francisco's first glass curtain-wall tower in the International Style, built just one year after Mies van der Rohe and Philip Johnson perfected the style in their Seagram Building on Park Avenue in New York City.

46_Headlands Center for the Arts

Using creativity as a weapon

The dramatic foothills, headlands, and bluffs to the north and south of San Francisco are filled with the ruins of military forts and fortifications. Beginning with the Spanish-American War, in 1898, there's been a long succession of increasingly powerful batteries and all that's left are bunkers and tunnels. In 1908, the army made a special effort to improve the coastal forts around the Golden Gate, and built Fort Barry, which became home base for the undertaking. It stands at the back of the Marin Headlands and can be reached by taking the road that winds up the bluffs facing the Golden Gate Bridge or else through a tunnel off the road to Sausalito.

Fort Barry was deactivated in 1950 and became part of the National Park Service in 1972. Ten years later, it was repurposed as the Headlands Center for the Arts (HCA), and major American artists including David Ireland and Ann Hamilton transformed the abandoned army barracks into studios and residences. Ireland is known for his site-specific installations using materials like paint cans, phone books, and the skull of a water buffalo. He and his crew stripped the military structure down to expose its historical layers, such as the stamped-tin ceilings, pillars, and sandblasted walls. Hamilton, a multimedia artist, was responsible for reshaping the former mess hall into the campus's main gathering place, where resident artists can share meals, ideas, and conversation.

The Headlands Center is open to the public, who can marvel at the transformation of the original buildings as well as attend artist exhibitions. Every year, 45 artists and writers from all over the world are awarded four- to ten-week residencies. The center also frequently offers guest lectures and open houses, giving visitors the opportunity to tour the residents' workspaces.

Address 944 Simmonds Road, Sausalito, CA 94965, +1 415.331.2787, www.headlands.org | **Getting there** Bus: 76X (Bunker Rd & Field Rd stop) | **Hours** Sun–Thu noon–5pm | **Tip** Rodeo Beach nearby offers good picnic sites and is ideal for kite flying or just watching the roaring Pacific.

47_Heath Ceramics

Very "Made in America"

Ceramicist Edith Heath (1911–2005) began producing her classic mid-century modern pottery in the Bay Area in 1947. Nearly 70 years later, Heath Ceramics is still crafting exquisite objects that are coveted by design addicts the world over – and anyone lucky enough to wander into one of their four brick-and-mortar showrooms. Edith Heath was an innovative technician as well as a designer, influenced by both the Bauhaus and native New Mexican potters. During World War II, when access to pottery wheels was scarce, she fashioned one herself from a treadle sewing machine, and built a kiln in her basement. Today, her work is included in collections at the MoMA and LACMA. She valued simple and durable goods, and believed in sustainable manufacturing. Much of her legacy is visible, along with her beautiful tableware and tiles, at Heath Ceramics' showroom in the Mission.

Heath's designs are distinguished by their clean lines, sensual textures, and understated palette of warm reds, slate grays, and watery blues. Tile is a Heath specialty and the myriad patterns and combinations presented form a dramatic visual backdrop to the retail space. Designers flock here to view the tile displays, which are frequently changing and always stunning.

In addition to the showroom, the Mission location includes Heath's tile factory. It's fascinating to see the dull slabs of clay flattened out and transformed into the exquisite wall and floor tiles. One can glimpse this taking place in the background, but for a more intimate understanding of the whole process, you can join one of the scheduled tours. There each step is demonstrated, from mixing the clay to cutting the shapes, to trimming, drying, glazing, firing, and stacking the tiles. It leaves you with a deep appreciation for the combination of industrial know-how and aesthetics that harks back to an era when "Made in America" was a stamp of great pride.

Address 2900 18th Street, San Francisco, CA 94110, +1 415.361.5552, www.heathceramics.com | **Getting there** Bus: 12 (Folsom St & 18th St stop); 33 (Potrero Ave & 18th St stop) | **Hours** Showroom Tue–Sat 10am–5pm, factory tours by reservation | **Tip** You can also visit the original Heath factory and showroom in Sausalito (400 Gate 5 Road), where all the tableware is crafted.

48 Hunter S. Thompson's House

Fear & Loathing in San Francisco

The house at 318 Parnassus Street that Hunter Thompson once called home is a two-story building that appears as anonymous and drab as Thompson was unique and colorful. But if only walls could talk …

Monsieur "Gonzo" defined a new kind of narrative journalism in which objectivity was blown to pieces and the writer became both protagonist and antagonist. Talese, Capote, Mailer, and Wolfe all had similar ideas about nonfiction novels, but Thompson took it a step further. His perspective was from the counterculture – defined as those angry, free young rebels who couldn't live with the establishment. Thompson himself was an outraged gun-carrying activist whose own credo was "I hate to advocate drugs, alcohol, violence, or insanity to anyone, but they've always worked for me."

In 1965, while living at 318 Parnassus, he spent a year getting tangled up in the dramatic world of the Hells Angels Motorcycle Club, which was run out of Oakland and led by Sonny Barger. Barger once famously said, "If I ever get too old to ride my motorcycle and have pretty girls, I'd rather just rob a bank and go back to prison." Thompson got up inside their lives and wrote it all down. His year of living dangerously ended with him on the receiving end of a brutal beating by the Angels. His publisher couldn't have been happier and his first book, *Hells Angels: The Strange and Terrible Saga of the Outlaw Motorcycle Gangs*, became a best seller.

Thompson used a gun to take his own life in 2005. His suicide note to his wife was published in *Rolling Stone* magazine: "No More Games. No More Bombs. No More Walking. No More Fun. No More Swimming. 67. That is 17 years past 50. 17 more than I needed or wanted. Boring. I am always bitchy. No Fun – for anybody. 67. You are getting Greedy. Act your (old) age. Relax – This won't hurt."

Address 318 Parnassus Street, San Francisco, CA 94117 | **Getting there** Bus: 6, 43 (Parnassus Ave & Willard St stop) | **Tip** Take a walk in the Cole Valley neighborhood. Above the awning of Crepes on Cole at 100 Carl Street, you can see the remains of the old sign for the Other Café, a comedy spot where Robin Williams and Dana Carvey performed before they hit the big time.

49 Hunter's Point

A flourishing artist colony in a shipyard

The shipyard at Hunter's Point dates back to 1870. At the beginning of World War II, the navy took it over and it was there, in July 1945, that key elements of the first atomic bomb were loaded on to the USS *Indianapolis* for delivery to Tinian Island, where, on August 6th, a B-29 bomber took off for Hiroshima. After the war, the navy's Radiological Defense Laboratory was established at Hunter's Point and it became the U.S. military's center for applied nuclear research. The facility closed in 1969 and in 1994, the navy shut down the entire 638-acre base, which had been listed as a Superfund site because of radioactive contamination. That atomic legacy still endures, along with other pollutants.

Still, the shipyard has been resilient, so much so that in 1983, a group of local artists created a colony among the old buildings that has, with enormous struggle, blossomed into a thriving community of more than 350 musicians, sculptors, painters, printmakers, digital artists, and writers. "The Point" is one of the largest artist collectives in the country. Studios are scattered throughout the warehouses, all in various states of decay. Rent is paid to the city. Lack of comforts aside, most of the shipyard residents are drawn by the novelty of the place, as well as its expansiveness and light. Twice a year, usually the last weekend in October and the first weekend in May, the artists open their studios to the public. These tours are a great opportunity for collectors and fans to meet the artists and experience their creative environments firsthand.

Today, the entire area around Hunter's Point is poised for redevelopment. When the renewal project is complete, hundreds of new houses will have been built, along with commercial ventures. Though most of the shipyard's structures will eventually be demolished and replaced, a brand-new building offering inexpensive artists' studios is planned.

Address Horn Avenue, San Francisco, CA 94124, +1 415.822.9675, www.shipyardartists.com | Getting there Bus: 19 (Galvez Ave & Horne Ave stop) | Hours Open Studios, one weekend every spring and fall, check website for dates and times | Tip On the way to Hunter's Point, note the medieval six-story stone tower of the Albion Castle at 881 Innes Street, the former home of the Albion Ale and Porter Brewery, founded in 1870 and closed in 1919. The castle's two underground caves are filled with fresh spring water. From 1928 to 1947 Albion Water Company bottled the drinking water. It's a private residence now.

50_Ingleside Terrace Sundial

Time is on its side

The city's southwestern neighborhoods, flowing across what used to be a vast ocean of sand dunes to the Pacific, share little in common with the Victorian splendor San Francisco is famous for. Stucco row houses and craftsmen bungalows line the windswept streets in these residential enclaves. And yet even "out here," a taste for the genteel and decorative spirit of the last century is kept alive in a secret park with a giant sundial.

Built in the westward expansion of the city after the earthquake of 1906, Ingleside Terrace was laid out around a popular old race-track for horses. In 1900, the track even played host to the first automobile race in California. The course later turned into Urbano Drive, and by 1912, more than 750 houses were planned for the loop, with the sundial park as a novelty centerpiece. In an effort to lure families to this new district, a tunnel was blasted through Twin Peaks for easy access from downtown, and a streetcar line was established. At an opening ceremony in 1913, the sundial was dedicated to two great recent building projects, the Twin Peaks Tunnel and the Panama Canal.

Turning off Urbano Drive, a smaller street, Entrada Court, leads like a spoke on a wheel to the circular park, where the giant 28-foot sundial slants elegantly upward. The dial resembles a slide, and indeed, generations of Ingleside children have employed it as such. On a fogless day, one can read the shadows along the clock face, with its Roman numerals marking the hours. Though the decorations on the surrounding "Grecian urns" are fading now, their symbolism representing the four ages of man, the four seasons of the year, and the four times of the day, would have been familiar to the neighborhood's original homebuyers. It is still a family-oriented community, with the annual Sundial Park Picnic in early fall, when local kids compete in circular "chariot races" on their bikes.

Address Entrada Court, Ingleside Terrace, San Francisco, CA 94132 | **Getting there** Light rail: K-Ingleside (Ocean Ave & Westgate Dr stop) | **Tip** A drive around Urbano Drive will take you back a century to the first classic car race in California.

51 Institute of Illegal Images

A "trip" to the museum

One literary entrance to the psychedelic sixties is Tom Wolfe's seminal nonfiction book, *The Electric Kool-Aid Acid Test* (1969). Wolfe, however, was from New York, and his take on counterculture was distinctly East Coast – as opposed to, say, Ken Kesey (author of *One Flew Over the Cuckoo's Nest*), who saw himself as a bridge between the Beats and the hippies, and who wrote and died in Oregon. In Acid Test, Wolfe interviews Kesey while in a San Mateo jail on drug charges. As Wolfe recounts, "He talked about something called the Acid Test and forms of expression in which there would be no separation between himself and the audience. It would be all one experience, with all the senses opened wide, words, music, lights, sounds, touch – *lightning*."

This is part of the background to consider as you step through the door of the Victorian on 20th Street in the Mission District known as the Institute of Illegal Images. It's also the home of Mark McCloud, who has assembled one of the world's largest collections of psychedelic art. The walls are jammed with 350 framed pieces, each displaying an illustrated blotter paper containing tabs of LSD. In its heyday, liquid LSD was poured in tiny amounts onto these absorbent perforated sheets and then individual "tabs" were placed under the tongue. The tabs here, however, have little or no potency left.

McCloud , who has been endlessly hounded by federal authorities, feels an obligation to portray the drug legacy of the 1960s "so maybe our children can better understand us" and to undo government stigmatization. Asked by Vice magazine how he got into collecting acid art, he told the interviewer, "See, I was a very difficult 17-year-old. Hendrix had just died, so I took 300 mikes of Orange Sunshine, and basically the fabric I existed on changed. I vibrated myself out of this world and into a different thing, and that's when I really started collecting."

Address 20th Street & Mission Street, San Francisco, CA 94110, www.blotterbarn.com | Getting there Bus: 14, 49 (Mission St & 22nd St stop) | Hours By appointment only; send an email to mark@blotterart.com | Tip Stop for a drink at Laszlo Bar, 2526 Mission Street.

52 The Interval at Long Now

For thinkers and drinkers

Fort Mason was a military base, first administered by the Spanish in 1776. When California became a state in 1850, the U.S. Army claimed it, and, during the Civil War, heavily fortified the place to resist Confederate attacks that never came. The fort was a major hub during World War II, but was eventually decommissioned in the 1970s, when it became part of the nation's first urban national park.

Since then, the center has evolved into a cultural enclave of dozens of small, mostly nonprofit organizations, museums, and theater companies, including the Magic Theater, where Sam Shepard began his career as the playwright-in-residence in 1975, and the Museo ItaloAmericano, which features a permanent collection of the work of well-known international painters such as Francesco Clemente.

Among this interesting group of establishments is the Long Now Foundation, which opened in 1996 and is guided by Stewart Brand, the original editor of the Whole Earth Catalogue. The foundation's charter is to "creatively foster long-term thinking and responsibility in the framework of the next 10,000 years." Projects include the building of a 10,000-year clock, a digital library of human languages, a seminar series on subjects that range from climate change to world conflict, and a collection of more than 3,000 books that are considered most critical to maintaining and/or rebuilding our society (should the need ever arise!), called the Manual for Civilization.

Nowadays these curious books are lining the two-story interior of the Interval, a techno utopian bar for thinkers and drinkers, opened by the Long Now Foundation in 2014. The constantly revolving soundtrack and "light painting" behind the bar was created by Brian Eno, one of the foundation's board members. The Interval is a simultaneous ode to the past, the present, and the future – a place where imagination, creativity, and cocktails happily coalesce.

Address 2 Marina Boulevard, Fort Mason Center, Building A, San Francisco, CA 94123, +1 415.561.6582, www.theinterval.org | **Getting there** Bus: 28, 28 L (Marina Blvd & Laguna St stop) | **Hours** Mon–Fri 10am–11pm, Fri & Sat 3–11pm | **Tip** Every Sunday morning year-round, you can shop for fresh fruits, vegetables, and delicious pastries at the small farmers market in the Fort Mason front parking lot.

53 Kabuki Springs & Spa

Wet, naked, and hot

Among the gifts Japanese immigrants brought to San Francisco when they arrived in the 1860s was the art of *sento*bathing. Perhaps an early ancestor of the California hot tub, the *sento*was (and is) a public bathhouse with facilities for both washing oneself and soaking communally with others of the same gender. It can be utilitarian, or in the case of Kabuki Hot Springs, luxurious.

While a modern steel pagoda marks the touristy public square in Japantown, or *Nihomachi*, the baths at Kabuki shelter a deeper Japanese sensibility. As you step through the doors and away from the busy traffic of Geary Boulevard, a tangible sense of aesthetic harmony and calm sets in. The bathing room is spacious and dimly lit, with wooden lounges placed strategically.

Distinct from other "spas," Kabuki retains a special communal vibe, which is reflected by the wide cross section of San Francisco residents who patronize the spa. On any given Friday the hot pool at Kabuki is likely to hold elaborately tattooed rock-star artists; Japanese women of all ages; mothers with their teenage daughters; and the waitress from next door, all soaking together – wet, naked, hot, and very quiet.

The baths are open to men or women on alternate days, with one co-ed day when bathing suits are required. Spotless, modern facilities include a hot and dry sauna, a cold plunge pool and the spacious hot pool with shallow seating, as well as Japanese bathing benches. An attendant makes sure the genmai tea, chilled face cloths, and other soothing amenities are well stocked and available. Guests can spend as long as they like in the baths and many choose to add on a traditional or Shiatsu massage, as well. The Shiatsu massage practioners, in particular, are among the city's best. When you're finished at Kabuki, all cleansed and relaxed, Japantown's myriad shopping and dining choices await you.

Address 1750 Geary Boulevard, San Francisco, CA 94115, +1 415.922.6000, www.kabukisprings.com | Getting there Bus: 22, 38, 38 L (Fillmore St & Geary Blvd stop) | Hours Daily 10am–10pm | Tip Just a short walk away is one of San Francisco's best restaurants – State Bird Provisions at 1529 Fillmore Street offers small dim sum-style plates of inventive and delicious dishes.

54 Landing at Leidessdorff

California's first Black millionaire

William Alexander Leidesdorff (1810–1848) was a prominent black entrepreneur and a key figure in the early development of San Francisco. Born in the Virgin Islands to a Danish father and a Creole mother, he embarked on a journey that led him to New Orleans before finally settling in Yerba Buena in 1841. At that time, this area, which would become San Francisco in 1847, was merely a quiet Mexican fishing village with around thirty families.

During his time in Yerba Buena, Leidesdorff made significant contributions, including helping to establish the city's first public school system as a member of the inaugural school board and serving as the first treasurer. He donated land for the school and aided in its construction. He also opened the first hotel and general store at Kearny and Clay Streets, as well as the first commercial shipping warehouse on what is now Leidesdorff Street near the Embarcadero. Notably, he was the first person to launch a steamboat on San Francisco Bay and was fluent in six languages.

In 1844, Leidesdorff was granted 35,000 acres of ranch land in the Sacramento Valley, now known as Folsom, by the Mexican government. A supporter of American annexation, he even borrowed against his property to finance American troops and supplies. His achievements earned him the title of the "African founding father of California." Tragically, he passed away suddenly at the age of 38 from "brain fever," just a year before the "gold rush" forever changed California.

Today, the city honors him with a street and a life-sized bronze statue at the intersection of Leidesdorff Street and Pine. A few blocks north, at the corner of Commercial, the "Landing at Leidesdorff" features a new mural celebrating his legacy. This area of the financial district has been revitalized with pop-up vendors, light shows, art events, and the nature-inspired restaurant and bar Heartwood.

Address Leidersdorff Street, San Francisco, CA 94104, www.downtownsf.org/go/landing-at-leidesdorff | Getting there Bus: 15 (Sansome St and Sacramento St stop) | Tip For a delicious meal and a refreshing drink, check out Heartwood, a bar and restaurant that captures the spirit of the Barbary Coast's early history alongside the stunning beauty of California's wilderness (531 Commercial Street, www.heartwood.com).

55 Lands End

A mystical walk through history

In one of the city's golden ages, in the late 1890s, Lands End was a Coney Island-like paradise of baths, booths, rinks, parks, a museum – and a seven-story chateau, which later became known as the Cliff House, perched precariously on the basalt bluffs above the ocean. Every weekend, people came to see the attractions, driving horse-drawn wagons over the sand dunes, or arriving on the nickel-a-ticket steam train that ran from California Street out through the Sea Cliff District.

It was all the brainchild of Adolph Sutro, the charismatic German who made his fortune with a state-of-the-art drainage tunnel that allowed miners deeper access to the Comstock Lode in the Sierras. Eventually, Sutro sold out and settled in San Francisco, where he built his estate above the Cliff House (see ch. 99).

There's a magnificent stroll through Lands End that begins across from Sutro Park, above the ruins of the baths and also the "Octagon House," which for years served as a lookout station. Using a system of telescopes and flags to indicate the kind of ship that was approaching, word was relayed from Lands End to the Presidio to Telegraph Hill, to the stevedores and taxi drivers waiting at the docks.

This walk, with its unforgettable views of the Marin Headlands and the Golden Gate Bridge, follows the route below the hospital and ends beneath the Legion of Honor. Halfway along you'll notice a sign for Eagle's Point, and a stairway winding down through the cypress trees to the beach. Partway down the stairs, there's a path leading to a wide precipice with a stone labyrinth. It was built in 2004 by local artist Eduardo Aguilera, whose work is tied to the theme of "peace, love and enlightenment." The site is particularly popular during equinoxes and solstices, which is in keeping with the fact that Lands End is partly a mystical place, and was once home to the indigenous Yelamu Ohlone people.

Address 608 Point Lobos Avenue, San Francisco, CA 94121, www.nps.gov/goga/planyourvisit/landsend.htm | **Getting there** Bus: 38, 38 L (48th Ave & Point Lobos Ave stop) | **Tip** For a longer hike, start from Sea Cliff, just below the Legion of Honor.

56 The Lefty O'Doul Bridge

In memory of a hometown hitter

The day shall live in baseball infamy: July 7, 1923. On that balmy evening at twilight, Francis "Lefty" O'Doul, playing for the Boston Red Sox, took the mound as a reliever in the first game of a double-header against the Cleveland Indians. O'Doul was up from the minors and that summer was his chance to scrawl his name on the walls of big-league heaven. But in that notorious sixth inning he set a record for the most runs given up by a relief pitcher in a single inning: 13. Earlier that season he set a record for the most batters faced in a single inning: 16. The final score was 27 to 3. Boston finished the season in last place in the American League and Lefty O'Doul went back down to the minors.

Lefty was converted into a power-hitting outfielder, and eventually returned to the majors in 1928. He was 31 and went on to become a two-time National League batting champion and was chosen for the Major-League Baseball All-Star Game in 1933. But there was more to come, a third act. When O'Doul retired as a player he became manager of the San Francisco Seals, helped develop Joe DiMaggio, and played a key role in popularizing baseball in Japan, where he's in the Hall of Fame.

In his honor, there's a pork-ribs restaurant and piano bar bearing his name just off Union Square. And then there's the Lefty O'Doul Bridge, also known as the Third Street Bridge, a massive and very efficient apparatus, just by AT&T Park. Opened in May 1933, it's one of four drawbridges in the city and was designed by Joseph Strauss, who also designed the Golden Gate Bridge (in fact, Charles A. Ellis designed the Golden Gate, but that's another story). It still works as perfectly as it did when it was first built, and opens for even the smallest sailboat traveling in and out of Mission Bay.

A fun fact for 007 fans: the bridge was seen in an exciting but brief car-chase sequence in the James Bond film *A View to Kill.*

Address 3rd Street at Mission Creek, San Francisco, CA 94107 | Getting there Light rail: T-Third (3rd St & 4th St stop) | Tip Take a stroll at nearby Cove Park. It is a well-maintained green space directly on the waterfront, with walking paths, lawns, and benches.

57_LeRoy King Carousel

Round and round we go

There are seven notable carousels in the Bay Area; three are in San Francisco. All were built around the turn of the 20th century. The carousel at the San Francisco Zoo was designed in 1921 by Gustav Dentzel, son of the famous German wagon and carousel maker, Michael Dentzel. In Golden Gate Park, behind Kezar Stadium, is a Herschell-Spillman carousel, built in 1914. It was originally steam powered and was a popular novelty in the 1939 World's Fair on Treasure Island.

And then there is the most glorious of the city's merry-go-rounds, forever spinning at the Children's Creativity Museum, in Yerba Buena Gardens. The LeRoy King Carousel was crafted by Charles I. D. Looff, the father of American carousels and the designer of the first carousel at Coney Island, in 1876. It was built in Rhode Island and originally intended to anchor a small amusement park on Market Street in San Francisco. But the earthquake in 1906 changed everything and the carousel ended up in Seattle's Luna Park. In 1913 it finally came to San Francisco, and for fifty years was the heart of Playland-at-the-Beach, which was the city's true Disneyland. After Playland closed in 1972, the carousel was snapped up by a collector and sat in storage until it was sold to Shoreline Village in Long Beach, California, in 1983, and eventually reappeared at Yerba Buena in 1998, where it remains housed in a glass rotunda to this day.

The carousel's recently restored collection of animals includes galloping horses, camels, leaping giraffes, rams, a lion, and two gilded chariots with blue and green dragons in the front. All the animals are distinguished by the ornate hand-carved artwork that marked carousels of the period. The horses, with their flowing manes, wear colorful bridles studded with bright jewels, and their tails are real horsehair. The cost for two rides is $4 per person or $3 with museum admission.

Address 221 4th Street, San Francisco, CA 94103, www.creativity.org/visit/childrens-creativity-carousel | Getting there Bus: 14, 14L (Mission St & 4th St stop) | Hours Fri–Sun 11:30am–4:30pm | Tip At the small Cartoon Art Museum (655 Mission Street) you'll find art ranging from early Peanuts drawings by Charles Schultz to the work of local contemporary cartoon artists.

58_Levi Strauss & Co.

Birthplace of the 501

Following the California Gold Rush, which began in January 1848, San Francisco turned minerals into machines. The city filled up with enterprises that included mills, shipyards, cattle yards, an explosives factory – and a dry-goods company that made bedding, purses, handkerchiefs, and clothing. That company was started by an oval-faced, never-married Bavarian named Levi Strauss.

Among Levi Strauss & Co.'s wholesale customers, there was a Russian immigrant and itinerant tailor named Jacob Davis. In the 1870s, Davis lived in Reno and one day a woman walked into his shop wanting work pants for her husband, a woodcutter. Davis responded with trousers made of "duck" cloth and heavy-duty cotton denim. The design included copper rivets for reinforcement, and a signature orange-threaded pattern stitched into the back pocket. These so-called "blue jeans" were instantly popular. Strauss helped Davis secure a patent in 1873 and devoted a factory to their production. The company was incorporated in 1890, and "waist overalls" were given the lot number 501.

Strauss died in 1902, and in 1906, the earthquake destroyed the company's headquarters and factories. But the business was quickly rebuilt at 250 Valencia Street – then a thoroughfare in a sleepy commercial district, now San Francisco's version of Abbot Kinney Boulevard in Venice, California.

The three-story timber-framed yellow building was the last Levi factory in this country, and closed in 2002. The building is now a Quaker elementary school. The floors of the original building remain, along with all the signs of wear. The reception desk is a Levi's prototype "retail desk." Note the large playground in front, which serves much the same purpose today as it always did, as a recreational area for children – once the children of company workers, now the children of families drawn to work in the "city in the cloud."

Address 250 Valencia Street, San Francisco, CA 94103 | **Getting there** Bus: 22 (16th St & Valencia St stop); 49 (Mission St & 14th St stop) | **Hours** Not open to the public, viewable from the street only | **Tip** The Levi Strauss Visitor Center is located at 1155 Battery Street and is open daily from 10am to 5pm; admission is free.

59_Lyon Street Steps

Where health meets wealth

Along the eastern edge of the Presidio, below the ridge that is the backbone of the Pacific Heights District, at the intersection of Lyon Street and Broadway, you come to what was originally a stairway street connecting the Heights with the Marina District below. These are known as the Lyon Street Steps – 244 of them in all, which drop down a steep hill through manicured hedges and flower gardens.

On your left as you descend is the Presidio, with its eucalyptus and redwood groves; on your right are some of San Francisco's most opulent mansions. Indeed, this is part of the city's "Gold Coast," (see ch. 15). Lords of the manors include former House Speaker Nancy Pelosi, philanthropist and composer Gordon Getty, and Oracle founder Larry Ellison – one of the new tech tycoons who are gradually changing not only the city's social strata but its charitable patterns, as well.

You come to the Lyon Street Steps for a feel of the city's Belle Époque, as well as a fabulous view of the bay, and perhaps for some good old-fashioned exercise. At any time of day, you will notice men and women in workout gear running and walking up and down the stairs with bags on their shoulders and buds in their ears. In that sense, the steps provide a selfie of the Northern California mindset when it comes to health and physicality.

Halfway down the stairs is an elegant garden dominated by a large gold heart sculpture, painted with a great red crane in flight. The installation is called *Migrant Heart* and was created by Hung Liu, a professor at Mills College in Oakland. It was unveiled in 2004 as part of a benefit program for the San Francisco General Hospital Foundation. About her creation, Liu wrote, "The crane is coming out of its shell to face a new world, like immigrants who come to the United States for a new start, while the gold backdrop is symbolic of hope."

Address Lyon Street between Broadway Street & Green Street, San Francisco, CA 94123 | **Getting there** Bus: 3 (Jackson St & Baker St stop); 41, 45 (Union St & Lyon St stop) | **Tip** You can walk straight down to the Palace of Fine Arts, the only structure from the 1915 Panama Pacific Exposition left on the original site.

60_Macondray Lane

Tales of the city

This is a walking city if there ever was one. How else could you discover the out-of-the-way little alleys, nooks, and steps that inevitably lead to those places where you say to yourself, "Ah, but if only I could live in *this* little bungalow! If only I could own *that* view, then … *then* my life would be perfect."

Forgetting that even if you could live on say, Macondray Lane – that secluded, charming cobblestone pedestrian path with the trellis at the Jones Street entrance and the cliff lined with densely overgrown rain-forest vegetation, with the towering eucalyptus and colorful flowers blooming beneath the trees and large dark green ferns on the north side of the hill, in a particular two-story modern townhouse, with a spickety-span minimalist design just by the little fountain with a waterfall and the Buddha statue, which offers a nearly 180-degree view of the city and the bay that includes such landmarks as Coit Tower, Alcatraz, and Fisherman's Wharf, and has a front entrance that looks like a bulkhead door in a submarine – even with all that, the truth is, your life would be much the same drama as it is now but with different sets and props.

You'll find the garden-lined Macondray Lane on top of Russian Hill, named after the Russian seamen buried there in the 19th century. Located between Union and Green Streets, it runs for two blocks. The most enchanting stretch, however, is between Jones and Taylor Streets, starting with the steep and narrow wooden steps ascending from Taylor.

San Francisco raconteur Armistead Maupin used Macondray Lane as a primary setting in his famous novel *Tales of the City*, albeit by another name: "The house was on Barbary Lane.… It was a well-weathered, three story structure made of brown shingles. It made Mary Ann think of an old bear with bits of foliage caught in its fur. She liked it instantly."

Address Macondray Lane, San Francisco, CA 94133 | **Getting there** Bus: 41, 45 (Union St & Leavenworth St stop) | **Tip** Take a stroll around the charming Russian Hill neighborhood, listen to the rumbling of the cable cars on Hyde Street, and stop for dinner at the highly rated Stones Throw (1896 Hyde Street).

61 The Malloch Building

For those who appreciate curves

The Malloch is that speeding ocean liner of a building at the top of Telegraph Hill, below Coit Tower near the Filbert Steps. It was built in 1937 and named after Jack and John Malloch, the father and son who developed it and claimed two units for themselves while renting out ten others. The architect was Irvin Goldstine, whose firm had offices in the city and down in Menlo Park. Little is known about him or his other work, but his building at 1360 Montgomery is a handsome expression of the style known as Streamline Moderne, which took off at the beginning of the 20th century in the imagination of the Italian architect and futurist, Antonio Sant'Elia. He was the one who drew up those fabulous colored renderings of cities to come, which became the inspiration for Fritz Lang's 1927 film, *Metropolis*, and Ridley Scott's 1982 cult classic, *Blade Runner*.

Every element in the Malloch exemplifies the Streamline aesthetic, such as a trio of silver sgrafittos by muralist Alfred Dupont. The building has been preserved exactly as it was when it was first built, including an open-air lobby that appears tropically lush and green, with Monstera leaves framed by sandblasted windows and Art Deco geometric images of clouds. There's also the original elevator, encased in a backlit glass brick shaft. And everywhere you look, there are curves. In each apartment, the dining room is round, the Art Deco fireplace is round, even the light seems rounded as it filters in through floor-to-ceiling windows, which, as you might imagine, offer unparalleled views of the Bay.

The building was used in the 1947 film *Dark Passage*, starring Lauren Bacall and Humphrey Bogart, about a man trying to clear his name of a murder charge. You can still admire the etched-glass windows and stylish railings just as they appear in the scene where Bacall leads Bogart up to her third-floor apartment, Number 10, for "the kiss."

Address 1360 Montgomery Street, San Francisco, CA 94133 | **Getting there** Streetcar: F-Line (The Embarcadero & Greenwich St stop) | **Hours** Private apartment building, courtyard is open | **Tip** Take a look at the fresco murals painted in the "social realism" style by 27 different artists at Coit Tower at the top of the Filbert stairs.

62_Maritime Museum

A "shipshape" exhibition space

At Fisherman's Wharf, below Ghirardelli Square and overlooking Aquatic Park, you come upon a building that resembles a great yacht. This is San Francisco's Maritime Museum, a striking architectural curio, with its Streamline Moderne style. Begun in 1936, it was a joint venture between the city and the New Deal Works Progress Administration (WPA), and intended as a public bathhouse. In the 1950s it was turned into a museum offering photographs and artifacts from the turn of the 20th century, an era when San Francisco's notorious red-light district, the Barbary Coast, had its heyday, and Jack London embodied the city's affection for the arts, the wilderness, and socialism.

But more than wharf history, the must-see here is the artwork, particularly the murals done by Hilaire Hiler and Sargent Claude Johnson. Hiler (1898–1966), whom Henry Miller once called a "hilarious painter whom I always think of with hilarious glee," was a true Renaissance character. He lived as an expat in Paris in the 1920s and then made his way to San Francisco. He is perhaps best remembered as an influential color theorist. His murals in the museum explore a fantastical undersea terrain, which at first glance have a childlike quality but upon closer study reveal the full extent of Hiler's vast imagination.

The other muralist represented at the museum is Sargent Claude Johnson (1888–1967), a celebrated black sculptor, ceramicist and painter. His more abstract murals were funded by the Federal Arts Project (FAP). In 1964, during the making of the museum's oral history, Johnson noted, referring to the FAP and WPA: "It's the best thing that ever happened to me because it gave me more of an incentive to keep on working … I thought about getting out of it because I come from a family of people who thought all artists were drunkards and everything else … but I think the WPA helped me to stay."

Address 900 Beach Street, San Francisco, CA 94109, +1 415.561.7100 | **Getting there** Bus: 19, 30, 47 (North Point St & Polk St stop) | **Hours** See website for hours and updates | **Tip** Stop for a famed Irish Coffee at the historic Buena Vista cafe, just across the street at 2765 Hyde Street.

63 Martin Luther King Jr. Memorial

A fountain for reflection in Yerba Buena Gardens

Every city has its "Times Square," that intersection of agora and neighborhood ego. San Francisco's center of identity is (arguably) on Mission Street between 3rd and 4th Streets in Yerba Buena Gardens. Its location and mood suggest a city that is – compared to, say, Manhattan – quieter, more laid-back and self-absorbed, less diverse and, despite its left-coast reputation, increasingly reserved.

If you're picnicking in Yerba Buena Gardens you may notice St. Patrick's Catholic church, standing defiantly in all its 19th-century glory, seemingly dwarfed by mile-high skyscrapers. In the midst of all this modernity, the church is a reminder that San Francisco remains a small town, somewhat Gothic and always brimming with huge ideas.

Yerba Buena Gardens is grounded by the Yerba Buena Center for the Arts (YBCA), which is noted for its community affiliations. The gardens, which are adjacent to the Moscone Center, incorporate various museums, including the Contemporary Jewish Museum, the Cartoon Art Museum, the Children's Creativity Museum, the Museum of the African Diaspora, and, across 3rd Street, the San Francisco Museum of Modern Art.

The centerpiece of Yerba Buena is *Revelation*, the city's Martin Luther King Memorial, a site-specific work built in 1993 as a collaboration between sculptor Houston Conwill, poet Estella Conwill Majozo, and architect Joseph DePace. The memorial is veiled behind a 50-foot-long wall of water, which flows down from a reflecting pool above. Along the corridor behind the waterfall are 12 glass panels with famous quotations from Dr. King. Each has been translated into various languages and dialects. With the sounds of the city drowned out, the site is an ideal place for reflection: a spot to contemplate, among other things, the whole notion of community.

Address 750 Howard Street, San Francisco, CA 94103, www.yerbabuenagardens.com | Getting there Bus: 14, 14 L (Mission St & 4th St stop) | Tip Soak up some sun and enjoy a great selection of teas at the Samovar Tea Lounge in Yerba Buena Gardens.

64 Mary Ellen Pleasant Park

California's mother of civil rights

A vest pocket park, in fact the smallest in the city, is set behind a low wall on the southwest corner of Bush and Octavia Streets. Look for the round plaque in the sidewalk that reads, "Mary Ellen Pleasant / Mother of Civil Rights in California / She supported the western terminus of the underground railway for fugitive slaves / This legendary pioneer once lived on this site and planted these six trees."

According to doyens with the San Francisco Ghost Tour, who gather in Mary Ellen Pleasant Park periodically, she haunts the eucalyptus trees here. But so much of what's known about Pleasant (1815-1904) is based on rumor, including the story that she was a voodoo queen and ran a bordello catering to a white clientele. What is verified, though, is that the park is on the place where she lived in a 30-room mansion.

When Pleasant, a wealthy Black woman and a widow, arrived in San Francisco from the East Coast in 1852, the Gold Rush was on. She possessed a refined talent for acquiring fortune and, well-to-do as she was, she worked as a servant in rich households, where she picked up investment tips. On a census form in 1890, she identified herself as a "capitalist by profession."

At the same time, she was a liberal activist and philanthropist. Having been a conductor on the Underground Railroad, she continued to help enslaved people get to California. She supported the local Black press, as well as the Athenaeum Building, a library and Black community center, and also the American Methodist Episcopal Zion Church. She once sued a streetcar company when a trolley wouldn't pick her up, even though there were plenty of seats and she had a ticket. The case went to the California Supreme Court, which ruled in her favor. Her political influence may also have helped overturn a law banning Black testimony in California courts. She's buried in a cemetery in Napa.

Address 1501-1699 Octavia Street, San Francisco, CA 94109 | Getting there Bus: 2 (Suter St & Octavia St stop) | Hours Unrestricted | Tip On the corner at 1801 Bush Street is the Healing Arts Building, which is filled with exotic therapists and spiritual healers.

65_Mavericks

A surfer's nirvana

South of San Francisco, within a 30-minute drive along the coast, is one of the world's most famous surfing spots. The site is actually two miles off shore, opposite a quirky little berg, Princeton-by-the-sea, which is just north of Half Moon Bay. Winter swells occasionally serve up spectacular Hawaii-sized waves that can top out at over 80 feet. For years, it was a nearly mythical place, since California is not known for huge waves. It's named after a white-haired German Shepherd named Maverick, who accompanied a group of local surfers that first discovered the spot, but deemed it too dangerous to surf, in March 1967.

The first person to surf Mavericks was a 17-year-old kid named Jeff Clark who had studied the massive waves carefully before making his first successful run in 1976. For the next 15 years Clark had Mavericks largely to himself. In 1990, the location started catching on and has been a surfer's tabernacle ever since. Apple's tenth major operating system, OS X Mavericks, released in 2013, is named after the spot. An annual invitation-only competition offers prizes running up to $150,000. However, some years the event – which is held as late as March – is forestalled by warming trends. AT&T Park, the home of the San Francisco Giants, usually offers live broadcasts on its 110-foot-wide video display.

The waves result from an unusual geological feature: a ramp of rock roughly 500 meters wide that runs toward the coast at Pillar Point and rises toward the surface. A trough lines either side of the ramp, which slows the wave down, and as it approaches the shallows, the wave splits and takes on a V-shape. The surfer has a choice of catching the wave to the right or the left. The left is more dangerous and less predictable. Mark Foo, one of the great proponents of the sport, drowned at Mavericks in 1994. His death was filmed in the surfing documentary, *Riding Giants*.

Address Pilar Point, Half Moon Bay, CA 94018, www.titansofmavericks.com | **Getting there** SamTrans: 17 (Avenue Alhambra & Vallejo St/Carmel Ave stop) | **Tip** Check out Jeff Clark's Mavericks Surf Shop at 25 Johnson Pier in Pillar Point Harbor.

66__Mechanics' Institute

Home to books and rooks

Located in the Beaux Arts building on Post Street in the busy financial district, just a short walk from bustling Union Square, is the quiet intellectual oasis of the Mechanics' Institute of San Francisco. It is one of several such organizations that appeared across the country in the late 19th century in an effort to help workers refine their trade skills. Opened in 1854 with a library to assist laid-off miners, the collection's technical focus has given way to literature, history, philosophy, finance, and hard-to-find periodicals. It's the oldest library on the West Coast.

In the lobby of this nine-story building is a wonderful mural – painted in dark, moody colors – designed by Arthur Mathews for the 1915 Panama-Pacific International Exposition. The lobby and staircase walls are wrapped in pink and black marble. The elegant iron spiral staircase ascends to the fourth floor, where you'll find a small and charming film-screening room, open to nonmembers. An ongoing feast of freshly popped popcorn and classic American and international films happens here every Friday.

The serene environment of the library, with its overstuffed armchairs surrounded by walls lined with bookcases, has the quality of an exclusive gentlemen's club. The Institute also hosts the longest continuously operating chess club in United States. The chess room, classically furnished with Thonet chairs surrounding the tables, is members-only, but you can enjoy a little gallery of photos documenting the club's history in the hallway. One of the club's students, Daniel Naroditsky, took the gold medal in the World Youth Chess Championship (for boys under 12) in 2007.

A private organization, it is open to the public for tours and viewing, but membership is required to check out materials from the library and participate in chess events. A free architectural tour is offered every Wednesday at noon.

Address 57 Post Street, San Francisco, CA 94104, +1 415.393.0101, www.milibrary.org | **Getting there** Bus: 2 (Post St & Montgomery St stop); 3 (Sansome St & Sutter St stop) | **Hours** Mon–Fri noon–6pm, Sat 10am–3pm | **Tip** At the intersection of Market Street and Geary Boulevard, you'll see Lotta's Fountain, commissioned by actress Lotta Crabtree in 1875. It served as an important meeting place after the big earthquake in 1906.

67 Mission Creek Houseboats

Islands in the storm

As you approach the city from the south on Highway 280, with the Bay View district to your right, the last exit before the highway ends leads up and over Mission Creek and lands you on Brannan and 6th Streets. It's as you reach the top of the elevated exit ramp that you might look down to your right and see a ragtag row of houseboats.

This eccentric neighborhood is known as Mission Bay District and has taken on new life recently due to a major redevelopment initiative by the city. In a wide creek, lined on one bank by million-dollar condos and on the other by furious construction work, there are about 20 houseboats moored to a long dock, which also accommodates conventional boats. This community of floating houses, which dates back to the 1960s, is a tiny neighborhood unto itself, with homes whose front and backyards consist of seawater. The houseboats have a long tradition of unconventional residents, including many artists and musicians, some of whom have lived there for several decades. But in recent years, with property prices skyrocketing, the city's deep-pocketed newcomers have come knocking.

The dock opened in the 1960s on Mission Creek, which carries water from underground wells in various parts of the Twin Peaks area to the San Francisco Bay. The houseboats are a motley collection of funky and fabulous. They range in styles and appearances from scrappy and very DIY to modern and industrial. One, for instance, is distinguished by its blue metal siding and tall loft-like casement windows.

A park with trees and a serpentine path runs along the bank and at the southern end there's a large enclosed vegetable garden. At night, while walking in the park with the sound of clanking halyards in the background, you may see some of the residents in their kitchens sitting down to dinner, as their boats roll to the rhythm of a deep sea.

Address Between 3rd Street & 4th Street on Mission Creek, San Francisco, CA 94107 | Getting there Light rail: T-Third (3rd St & 4th St stop) | Tip Take a stroll to UCSF park and check out Richard Serra's sculpture Ballast, consisting of two 50-foot-tall Cor-Ten steel plates.

68 Mission Dolores Cemetery

Where the bodies are buried

Cities often conceal their origins (and sins) under layers of concrete and urban renewal, but just beyond the white adobe walls at Mission Dolores the evidence is in plain sight. Visitors enter the grounds through a small room adjoining the original Mission Chapel. Built in 1781, it is by far the oldest building in the city.

The cemetery is situated in a courtyard behind the chapel, thick with rosebushes, twisted old trees, and stone walkways. A statue of Mission founder Junipero Serra stands sentinel, but his head is bowed as if in sorrow. Thousands of Native Californians are buried here, including the Miwok and Ohlone converts who first built the missions, some of their own free will, though many not. A replica of an Ohlone hut in one corner of the cemetery pays them homage.

Names on the worn gravestones echo the progress of California history: there is Luis Antonio Arguello, the first Mexican governor; Francisco De Haro, the first mayor; and Sanchez, a wealthy don of the rancho era, among others. Mexico ceded its lands in Alta California to the United States in 1848, just in time for the Gold Rush era. The appearance of Irish and English names on the gravestones reflects this transition.

Three graves, set apart with wrought-iron railings, belong to Cora, Casey, and Sullivan, victims of the "Vigilance Committee" – a vigilante group that sought to impose order in the crime-infested boomtown of the 1850s. Sullivan, a crook and a pugilist, worked guarding ballot boxes for corrupt politicians. Some say he slit his own wrists in the vigilante prison; others claim that he was murdered. His epitaph reads: *Remember not, O Lord, our offenses, nor those of our parents. Neither take thou vengeance of our sins....* Which provides a fitting comment on the history of San Francisco in general.

Address 3321 16th Street, San Francisco, CA 94114, www.missiondolores.org/old-mission/visitor.html | **Getting there** Light rail: J-Church (Church St & 16th St stop); Bus: 22 (16th St & Dolores St stop) | **Hours** Tue–Sun 10am–4pm | **Tip** Sample one of the best homemade ice creams in San Francisco at Bi-Rite Creamery at 3692 18th Street. You can choose from many exotic flavors, like orange cardamom and honey lavender.

69 Mission Dolores Park

Just chillin' at DP

Its proper name is Mission Dolores Park, but it's often simply referred to as 'Dolores' or 'DP.' When you think of a park, you usually think of the color green, right? Well, on a sunny day at Dolores, the green is covered, and San Francisco's true colors come out. Imagine 10,000 people stretched out on a 14-acre hillside with a perfect view of the city's skyline in the distance.

The park is located between 18th and 20th Streets with the Mission District to the East and the Castro to the West. Prior to the arrival of the Spanish missionaries, the area was inhabited by Native Americans of the Yelamu tribe. In the 19th century, the land was used as a Jewish cemetery. But at the turn of the century, cemeteries were forbidden in the city, and the plot of land officially became a park. Since then, it has become an historic go-to spot for the city's eclectics, the Mission's Latino population, local hipsters, young families, and the LGBTQ community. Some locals even call the park San Francisco's "real" beach. Dolores is home to Cinco de Mayo celebrations, the Pride Parade, a 'Hunky Jesus' competition every Easter Sunday, and "just chillin'" kinds of afternoons.

Only San Francisco's beautifully diverse and uniquely liberal community could so many people come together in such a small space and simply enjoy a sunny day in total peace and happiness. Dolores gear includes - but is not limited to - blankets, boom boxes, dogs, friends, food, and games. Joints and drinks are the norm as well, but just remember: no glass allowed! If you need to restock on snacks, a foodie's paradise lies at the north-west corner of the park on 18th street. Some notable stops are Tartine, arguably the best bakery in the city; Delfina, a delicious pizzeria; and Bi-Rite, SF's beloved ice cream shop. Expect a line at all these places. (Note: the sweeter the food, the longer the line.)

Address 19th Street and Dolores Street, San Francisco, CA 94110, www.sfrecpark.org/destination/mission-dolores-park | **Getting there** Lightrail: J-Church (20th St stop) | **Hours** Daily 6am–10pm | **Tip** Mission San Francisco de Asís, or Mission Dolores, is the oldest surviving structure in San Francisco, built in 1776 (3321 Sixteenth Street, San Francisco, CA 94114, www.missionscalifornia.com/mission-facts/san-francisco-de-asis).

70 Modernism

High Culture in Little Saigon

Many San Franciscans have been talking for quite some time about the "Faustian Pact" the city has made with Silicon Valley empires. A long-time resident was quoted in *The Washington Post* as saying, "I still love my town... but it's quite harsh and quite brutal and it frightens me." No doubt the sentiment is genuine, but the reality may not be as depressing and as it might appear.

There has indeed been an exodus of artists, trade workers, and teachers. Those who remain, other than coders, include philanthropists, high-end artists, "creatives," and people like art dealer Martin Muller, a beloved figure in art circles. Modernism is his 5,000 square-foot gallery on Ellis Street, in the Little Saigon District, one and a half block east of Van Ness. The space was designed by Aidlin Darling, whose work includes a "spiritual refuge" at Stanford University. The Modernism gallery is a must-see.

In the Fall of 1979, Swiss-born Muller opened Modernism in San Francisco with an international roster of artists. Forty years later, the gallery has presented a broad range of contemporary artworks from non-objective (the colorful canvases of Charles Arnoldi and Naomie Kremer) and conceptual (the urban archaeology of affichiste Jacques Villeglé and the provocative socio-political paintings of Gottfried Helnwein), to representational (the paintings conveying the existential essence of scenes from everyday life by John Register, the iconic Pop Art paintings of Mel Ramos, and the challenging Feminist photography of Judy Dater). The contemporary program is complemented by a stream of historical exhibitions, primarily of early 20th century European and eastern Avant- Garde movements, including the Russian Avant-Garde 1910-1930, Dada, Cubism, Surrealism, and German Expressionism.

Muller describes himself as an "independent spirit with endless curiosity about new artistic ideas."

Address 724 Ellis Street, San Francisco, CA 94109, +1 415.541.0461, www.modernisminc.com | Getting there Bus: 31 (Eddy & Larkin St stop), then walk 1 block to Ellis Street | Hours Tue–Sat 10am–5:30pm | Tip For New Orleans-style deliciousness, walk over to Brenda's French Soul Food (652 Polk Street, San Francisco, CA 94109, www.frenchsoulfood.com).

71 The Monastery Stones

Relics in the Botanical Garden

Golden Gate Park is filled with hidden treasures, not least the 55-acre botanical garden, formerly known as the Strybing Arboretum. It opened in 1940 off 9th Avenue, and was laid out largely by that portly and imperious superintendent of the park, that genius, John McLaren, who'd begun his career anchoring dunes on the estuary along Scotland's River Forth. In San Francisco, he set out the dimensions of the park, and to protect it from the ocean, he used whatever he could find in the way of city debris to build the berm that's now the Great Highway.

Whether you care about horticulture, the arboretum is nearly a sacred space. It's filled with meadows, glades, and winding paths running through a succession of gardens. In one area, you'll find one of the largest collections of magnolias in the world. In another – the California native garden – are species from the state's different landscapes: meadowfoam from the arroyos, dutchman's pipe from the woodlands, and matilija poppies from the chaparrals of southern California. And then there's a Mesoamerican cloud forest with tree daisies and fuchsias. All told, there are some 8,000 plant species.

Throughout the arboretum are beautifully cut stones, which are among the 1000 taken from Santa Maria de Ovila, a Spanish monastery built 90 miles northeast of Madrid in 1181. In 1835, the Spanish government confiscated the property, along with 900 other monasteries, and sold them to private owners, who often used them as barns. In 1930, William Randolph Hearst, the American publisher, brought the stones from Santa Maria de Ovila to California where he hoped to use them to build yet another castle after San Simeon, at a property up the coast called Wyntoon. But the Depression intervened, and in 1941, the city acquired the stones. Now they stand – some still with markings by medieval stonemasons – like quiet odes to Ozymandias.

Address 1199 9th Avenue, San Francisco, CA 94122, www.sfbotanicalgarden.org | Getting there Bus: 44, 71, 71 L (9th Ave & Lincoln Way stop) | Tip The Botanical Garden is a perfect place to bring a picnic and a blanket and just enjoy.

72__Moraga Street Steps

Stairway to Heaven

The Moraga Street Steps are an inspired example of site-specific art that "elevates" its surroundings into something magical, yet intensely local at the same time. Part of this chemistry comes from the view of the Pacific Ocean that glitters in the distance, and then seems to start crawling up the flight of 116 steps. A tile mosaic begins at the base of the stairs with scenes deep under the ocean, progresses upward to the water's surface, climbs onto land, into the air, and just as one nears the top of the steps and the actual sky appears, the scene changes to outer space and finally the sun. It's a powerful commingling of form and content. Climbing the stairs, one ascends from submarine to the heavenly heights, both visually and physically, as the overall design is revealed step by step. Along the way the polished colors of the tiles vibrate with life in the bright western light. Beautiful gardens along the slope add to the riot of living forms.

The mosaic was created by local artists Aileen Barr and Colette Crucher, who collaborated on both its design and fabrication. Unique in this mosaic are 2,000 handmade tiles in the shape of fish, animals, flowers, birds, and stars, many inscribed with the names of neighborhood sponsors and volunteers. Each of these brilliantly hued tiles is an artwork in itself. And every one of the 163 panels on the vertical step risers is intricate enough to stand on its own.

The stairs, which ascend from 16th Avenue to 15th Avenue, have been in place since the 1920s but originally had no decoration. The mosaic was completed in 2005 with the city's blessing and the help of more than 300 area volunteers, including a local tile company that provided the final installation.

The creators were inspired in part by the Escaderia Selarón in Rio de Janeiro, and have now brought their work to several other public stairway projects in the city.

Address 1700 16th Avenue, San Francisco, CA 94122, www.tiledsteps.org | **Getting there** Bus: 66 (16th Ave & Moraga St stop) | **Tip** At the top of the steps, turn right onto 15th Avenue and you'll find a smaller wooden staircase that will take you up to a hilltop park, aptly named Grandview. The panoramic vista of the Outer Sunset avenues marching to the beach, with the great green rectangle of Golden Gate Park along the edge, is particularly nice at dusk.

73 Musée Mécanique

A penny arcade on the Embarcadero

In an era when retro is the new cool, there's no finer, more evocative time machine than the Musée Mécanique, which you'll find in an old warehouse on Pier 45, close to Fisherman's Wharf. It's a showcase for hundreds of coin-operated machines dating back to the 19th century, and one of the largest collections of its kind in the world. The Musée captures that particular form of magic – the kind made from sprockets, cogs, levers, and pulleys – that spun out of the industrial revolution. Its roots, however, go back to the compelling illusion of the Mechanical Turk. First exhibited in 1770, the Mechanical Turk appeared to be an automated chess-playing device with a mind of its own, when in fact, a human chess master was hiding inside the cabinet, controlling every move.

At Musée Mécanique the magic is entirely mechanical. The machines, which need constant maintenance, cost a quarter. You can play music or baseball, or find out your fortune. There are "love testers" and a Mutoscope with a peep show that reveals the "secret lives of belly dancers." Many of the machines include elaborate dioramas and some are made from toothpicks and were built by prisoners at Alcatraz. Of special interest to people in San Francisco is the six-foot-tall lady named Laughing Sal, with her bloodcurdling chortle. There are also a variety of nostalgic pinball machines and vintage video games from the eighties and nineties.

The idea for this museum began in the imagination Ed Zelinsky (1922–2004), who became transfixed by mechanical intricacies when he was a boy, and went on to amass a collection of over 300 coin-operated games and amusements. For years the exhibit was a fixture at Playland, the city's beloved former amusement park. Playland closed in 1972 and the Musée found a new home in the Cliff House basement. In 2002 it was moved to Pier 45. Admission is free; the machines are not.

Address Pier 45, Shed A, San Francisco, CA 94133, +1 415.346.2000, www.museemecaniquesf.com | Getting there Streetcar: F-Line (Jefferson St & Taylor St stop); Bus: 39 (Powell St & North Point St stop); 47 (North Point St & Mason St stop) | Hours Mon–Fri 10am–7pm, Sat & Sun 10am–8pm | Tip Aquatic Park, with its small sandy beach, is a nice spot to enjoy some sun, check out the boats, or watch the Dolphin Club members swimming without wetsuits in the chilly Bay waters.

74_National Cemetery Overlook

A graveyard with a view

The Presidio was established in 1776 by the Spanish, who occupied it as a settlement until 1822, when it fell under Mexican rule. The U.S. Army then took control in 1846, and it became a staging zone for many of the country's major conflicts. Its military heritage ended with the Sixth Army's deactivation in 1994. Two years later the Presidio was privatized. Many of the former barracks have since been remodeled and leased to the public. Among the tenants are Lucasfilm; the charming Walt Disney Family Museum; and some lovely eateries, such as the Presidio Social Club.

For a visitor there are dozens of places in the Presidio worth seeing, but one that bears singling out is the San Francisco National Cemetery, which was established in 1884 and remains a great historical landmark, as well as a place for reflection and renewal. The National Cemetery Overlook, hidden among the eucalyptus trees above the steep manicured green slope dotted with white grave markers, also offers unparalleled views of the bay and Golden Gate Bridge.

Among those buried here are the likes of Buffalo Soldier and Medal of Honor winner William H. Thompkins, and the Union general Irvin McDowell, who famously lost the first major battle of the Civil War. There are also the graves of two very interesting women. One was "Miss Major" Pauline Cushman, a stage performer who became a Union spy. Later, P. T. Barnum featured her among his circus acts. She died in 1893 in San Francisco, down and out, and alone. The other woman is the "Great Western," Sarah Bowman, who stood six feet tall, had red hair, and wore pistols. She served as a nurse in the Mexican wars, later ran a brothel in El Paso, and in 1866, died of a spider bite in Fort Yuma, Arizona. She was buried with full military honors in Yuma, and was later reinterred at the Presidio.

Address 462-498 Nauman Road, San Francisco, CA 94129, www.presidio.gov/explore/trails/Pages/national-cemetery-overlook.aspx | **Getting there** Bus: 28 L, 43 (Letterman Dr & Lincoln Blvd stop) | **Tip** Take the dramatic Batteries to Bluffs Trail, which leads you along the cliffs of the Pacific Ocean all the way to Marshall's Beach. The views are spectacular.

75 Nimitz Mansion

Secret views from Yerba Buena

San Francisco has always been a Navy town, and still celebrates its heritage once a year with a roar-and-soar performance by the Blue Angels, a six-jet naval precision flying team. Indeed, the area's naval legacy extends throughout the bay, from the Hunter's Point shipyard in San Francisco, to the Mare Island yards in Vallejo, both long closed; to the naval air station in Alameda, where the WW II aircraft carrier USS *Hornet* is moored and is now a terrific museum; to Moffett Field in Sunnyvale, once home to Cold War submarine hunters and soon to become Google's new headquarters.

And then there is Yerba Buena Island, which stands as an anchor point for the two spans of the Bay Bridge, and is a longtime military area. It's connected by a short causeway to Treasure Island, and now includes various Coast Guard facilities, an operational home for the Department of Homeland Security, and below the new eastern half of the bridge at the intersection of Whiting Way and Garden Way, Quarters One, otherwise known as the Nimitz Mansion. In fact, it's less a mansion than a fancy and fanciful officer's house. Designed in the Classical Revival style, complete with double Ionic columns, it was built in 1900 as the naval station's commandant's residence.

From the green grounds that sweep down to the bay in front of the white wood frame house, you are presented with the striking view of the Bay Bridge, and Oakland in the background. The estate is surprisingly quiet despite the traffic overhead, and the long vistas are befitting what was once home to one of America's greatest naval heroes, Chester K. Nimitz, a fleet admiral during World War II and a superb tactician who orchestrated critical victories at Midway and Leyte Gulf.

These days the mansion, with its plantation airs, is used for Halloween parties or weddings under the cherry tree in the formal gardens.

Address 1 Whiting Way, Treasure Island, San Francisco, CA 94130 | Getting there Bus: 108 (Treasure Island Rd Guard Station stop) | Tip The grounds are perfect for enjoying a Sunday picnic with a view of the Bay Bridge.

76 The Observation Tower

A castle in the trees at the de Young

If you're walking (or driving) along JFK Drive in Golden Gate Park, at about Ninth Avenue you might notice a looming metal tower rising amidst the lush canopy of evergreens. The tower, clad in an exoskeleton of reddish copper, resembles a castle battlement. Follow the tower to its base, through a sculpture garden, behind the trees, and you come to the de Young Museum, one of the Bay Area's largest fine art museums and one that mixes natural and manmade aesthetics with abandon and flourish.

When the de Young Museum was rebuilt after the Loma Prieta earthquake in 1989, the architectural firm of Herzog and de Meuron, with San Francisco's Fong and Chen Architects, set out to use natural materials, such as copper, wood, stone and glass in its design. Some residents adore the ultra-modern reconstruction; others prefer the original Beaux-Arts-style building that was torn down.

Regardless of taste, the observation floor is a unique pleasure. An elevator rises 144 feet to the 360-degree viewing area, which is ringed by a full circle of tall windows. The tower just clears the tallest trees in the park, so that the panoramic vistas are framed by the lush greenery and swaying eucalyptus boughs below.

From this airy vantage point, it feels as if you are viewing San Francisco from a very high tree house. The landscape of the park flows out in all directions. To the east, the living roof of the Academy of Sciences undulates like the hillside just behind it. To the west, the view stretches all the way to the Marin Headlands and the Golden Gate Bridge – which appears strangely close, partly because it rises above the city to about the same elevation.

Visitors can pinpoint other landmarks throughout the city using the giant aerial photographs posted along the base of the windows. Admission to the Hamon Tower Observation Level, located in the east wing of the museum, is free to visitors.

Address de Young Museum, 50 Hagiwara Tea Garden Drive, San Francisco, CA 94118, +1 415.750.3600, www.deyoung.famsf.org | Getting there Bus: 44 (Academy of Sciences stop) | Hours Tue–Sun 9:30am–5pm | Tip Every Sunday during the summer, the Golden Gate Park Band gives free concerts in the Music Concourse and Pavilion, located in front of the de Young Museum.

77_Ocean Beach

Hanging ten on city waves

At the western end of the city, across the Great Highway, you come upon Ocean Beach, which stretches from below the Cliff House south more than three miles to the bluffs that mark the beginning of Fort Funston. The beach, which is part of the Golden Gate National Parks Conservancy, is wide and occasionally wild, including the part between Lincoln and Sloat, which is filled with dunes, tall grass, and the endangered western snowy plover. The section between Lincoln and Noriega is a particularly fond place for picnics, kiting, relationship makeovers, and sunset viewing.

To the north, the section between Lincoln and the Cliff House bluffs is more public bath and spectacle. Fires are permitted, and on warm nights – rare during summer months – the beach and boardwalk are covered over in hipsters and teen angels. There's a highly recommended bar down behind Beach Chalet, the large two-story building that presides over this part of the beach. Dogs are allowed off the leash along some parts of Ocean Beach, for example at the Great Highway and Fort Funston.

The beach is popular among surfers, especially those who don't have time to drive down the coast to Half Moon Bay, to Mavericks, or who prefer smaller sets. Favorite spots are at the foot of Sloat Boulevard or Lawton Street, or else below the Cliff House, although that's rocky and inadvisable. The best times to surf are the mornings and the best place to park is on the Little Great Highway, which runs parallel to the Great Highway. The riptides are legendary, and if caught in one, the recommended strategy is to swim parallel to the beach until you get out of it. There are occasional lifeguards, and both surfers and swimmers are advised to keep them in sight. Sharks have been spotted over the years, including great whites, although this is a much quieter beach than, say, Stinson Beach, across the Golden Gate Bridge in Marin.

Address Ocean Beach, Golden Gate National Recreation Area, San Francisco, CA 94122 | Getting there Bus: 31 (Cabrillo St & La Playa St stop); 16X, 71, 71L (Ortega St & 48th Ave stop); Light rail: N-Judah (Judah & La Playa St stop), L-Taravel (Wawona St & 46th Ave stop) | Tip A sunset walk on Ocean Beach is a must. The coast is often windy and cold, so wear plenty of layers.

78__ODC

Put on your dancin' shoes

San Francisco is a dance town. There are a half-dozen professional ballet companies alone, as well as several contemporary companies and a conservatory. And then there's the Oberlin Dance Collective, known as ODC, in the Mission District. Founded in 1971 by Brenda Way, who trained with Balanchine, it has become a nationally recognized modern dance company and is considered one of the great "dance incubators" in the country, as well.

What drives ODC is the way it interacts with the community, through performances, but also through its many dance classes and workshops. All classes are led by professional dancers who invariably have their own companies or perform at other venues. Classes, which take place in one of five studios, are open to all levels and to one-time visitors. Two of the studios are large enough to handle 100 dancers at a time. Beyond specialized classes in salsa and Latin, jazz, Indian, and African dance, there's a core class, called Rhythm and Motion, which attracts people of all ages who like to dance and work out at the same time. The accompanying music is an eclectic mix of hip-hop, pop, jazz, and other styles. Each song has its own choreography, which draws from a complete dance vocabulary, and remains the same no matter the teacher. There is no set of rules about "how you're supposed to dance."

Interestingly, these classes have been so successful that they largely finance the company, along with their two-building campus on Shotwell Street. ODC's involvement with the community extends to organizing highly choreographed flash mobs, along with participating in the Gay Pride parade and Carnival, one of the city's great spring festivals.

The professional company has a varied repertoire, including a terrific holiday version of *The Velveteen Rabbit*. The center has a cafe and a library, and introductory classes are free.

Address 351 Shotwell Street, San Francisco, CA 94110, +1 415.549.8519, www.odc.dance | **Getting there** Bus: 12 (Folsom St & 18th St stop) | **Hours** See website for class and performance schedules | **Tip** The Stable Cafe on 17th and Folsom Street was originally the carriage house of San Francisco's mayor in 1870, and is now a great place for coffee.

79__Old Skool Café

Serving up second chances

California prisons are notoriously overcrowded, to the point where an increasing number of "lifers" are being released, along with many less dangerous felons. The inmate population at San Quentin, located just 15 minutes from San Francisco in Marin County, is at 130 percent of capacity. It also holds more than 700 men on death row, the most of any state in the country. However, whether there will be more executions in California remains unclear.

Naturally, parolees released from San Quentin often stop in San Francisco; some disappear among the homeless; others look for work, especially at the Delancey Foundation, founded by Mimi Silbert, one of the city's iconic characters for the last 40 years. She's best known for starting a first-rate restaurant on the Embarcadero where waiters include many ex-convicts and former drug addicts. Ms. Silbert has started several other enterprises in the city as well, including a furniture business, a moving company, and a bookstore. And she does it all without government funding or a professional staff.

Following in the footsteps of Silbert and the Delancey Foundation, there's the Old Skool Café, a youth-run 1940s-style supper club serving up Southern food in the Bay View District. It was started by Teresa Goines, a former juvenile corrections officer who believes the best way to keep kids out of prison is to get them a job where they can accomplish something. Old Skool provides training and employment to 21 at-risk kids between the ages of 16 and 22. The cafe sports swanky red leather booths and elegant chandeliers.

Entertainment is provided by a rotating group of young jazz musicians, many from SFJAZZ. The waiters, who sport crisp red shirts, black bow ties, suspenders, and fedoras, openly share their life stories with diners.

The cafe program's motto is, quite aptly, "Come hungry. Leave inspired."

Address 1429 Mendell Street, San Francisco, CA 94124, +1 415.822.8531, www.oldskoolcafe.org | **Getting there** Bus: 54 (3rd St & Palou Ave stop); Light rail: T-Third (3rd St & Oakdale Ave stop) | **Hours** Thu–Sat 5–9pm | **Tip** The Bay View Opera House – the oldest opera house in San Francisco – is around the corner at 4705 3rd Street.

80_The Parrots of Telegraph Hill

As free as a bird

Among the city's novelties are various steps and stairways. Some are so steep you have to smile, particularly those on Russian Hill and even more so on Telegraph Hill around Coit Tower. It's hard to imagine having to climb these steps every day. The truth is that city residents use these staircases more for exercise than getting to and fro; meanwhile, tourists come to see the surrounding lush gardens, the quaint cottages, the spectacular views, and the occasional art pieces.

The two most dramatic stairways ascend from Sansome Street, just off the Embarcadero at Levi's Plaza, and wind up to Coit Tower. Each has more than 400 steps. One is the Greenwich Steps – not to be confused with the Greenwich Steps on Russian Hill. The other is the Filbert Steps, which, in addition to other sights and sounds, is home to a famous flock of wild parrots.

There are at least two groups of parrots in the city. One moves around Golden Gate Park; the other roosts along Napier Lane, just off the Filbert steps. The Filbert flock is comprised of perhaps 30 to 40 cherry-headed conures from South America. How they got to San Francisco isn't clear. According to one account, a crazy old pet store owner simply opened all the birdcages and windows one day.

The Filbert flock was captured in Judy Irving's documentary *The Wild Parrots of Telegraph Hill.* The 2003 film profiles a homeless musician named Mark Bittner, who lived in the neighborhood and spent five years interacting with the birds. He begins his narrative: "It wasn't a plan. It just happened. I hadn't expected it to go this far ..." What he hadn't anticipated was the strength of his bond as he began to reject that urban notion that animals somehow can't experience pain. In fact, says Bittner, "they're afraid of injury, they're afraid of death, they're afraid of being alone. Like us."

Address Greenwich Steps & Filbert Steps, San Francisco, CA 94133 | **Getting there** Streetcar: F-Line (Embarcadero & Greenwich St stop) | **Tip** The steps are easily accessible from Levi's plaza, a great little picnic spot just next to Levi Strauss & Company's world headquarters.

81__Patricia's Green

From parkway to park

There's a vest-pocket park at the corner of Hayes and Octavia that has become a beacon of sorts for the vibrant little neighborhood that surrounds it. Twenty-five years ago, however, this area was decidedly un-charming. It was riddled with crime and dominated by the hideous double decker Central Freeway, which fed and drained western parts of the city each day. Then on October 17, 1989, the 6.9 Loma Prieta earthquake struck, collapsing roads and bridges all over the Bay Area, including sections of the Central Freeway.

In the decade that followed, a Hayes Valley activist named Patricia Walkup rallied supporters who went door-to-door convincing local residents to sign petitions to replace the freeway's remains with a public green space and a more attractive access route through the neighborhood. Her hard work contributed to the creation of Octavia Boulevard, a major tree-lined roadway, and Patricia's Green, an urban park named after Walkup, featuring picnic tables, benches, a playground, and a series of art installations that are curated by Burning Man artists. This little outdoor haven has become the center of one of the most revitalized and lively areas of San Francisco, which includes the War Memorial Opera House and Davies Hall just down the street.

In addition, within a block or two in either direction from the park, you'll find some of the city's best restaurants and shops, along Hayes Street. Many of the retailers are high end, but these are not chain stores, and each offers unique products, such as custom handmade corsets and exquisite leather goods.

One of the coolest features of the neighborhood is an innovative development project called Proxy, which hosts a rotating roster of temporary shops and restaurants housed in renovated shipping containers. The project has expanded to include pop-up food trucks and, more recently, an outdoor movie theater.

Address Hayes Street & Octavia Street, San Francisco, CA 94102 | Getting there Bus: 21 (Laguna St & Hayes St stop) | Tip Amano on Hayes Street is a heaven for a good Italian fare.

82 The Phoenix Hotel

Rock 'n' roll crash pad

The Tenderloin District, long the bad-boy part of town, is gentrifying. For better and for worse, some measure of diversity is being lost. The "better" is that the city is ever so slowly replacing the old SRO hotels, those firetraps for residents living on Public Assistance and forgotten medications, where the night porter grimaces behind the bulletproof glass inside a heavy metal cage in the lobby. In other ways, little has changed. This is the most ethnically and sexually diverse district in the city, and is still home to schizophrenics screaming from the rooftops, addicts shot up and half dead in Boeddeker Park, and the same old faces cued up outside St. Anthony's Dining Room on Golden Gate Avenue next to Saint Boniface Church. The last large-scale free food source left in the city, it serves 2,700 people a day. It's all a puddle of clouded humanity gradually drying up from the edges.

Of course, there are more mainstream gems in the Tenderloin: certain restaurants, cafes, clubs, churches, and hotels. And there are still echoes of the old Barbary Coast, when this whole neighborhood was the city's Cotton Club. One of these is the Phoenix Hotel, on Eddy Street at Larkin. The neon sign reads, "Hotel, Restaurant, Cocktails." At a glance, it looks like a 1970s roadhouse in the San Fernando Valley. But there's also a tropical vibe and a kind of sensuousness. It bills itself as a motor lodge, but seems vaguely like a California version of the Chelsea Hotel in Manhattan, a local curio with a retro-chic vibe, which has served as a rock 'n' roll crash pad for musicians such as Pearl Jam, the Killers, and the Red Hot Chili Peppers.

These days, clients also include well-heeled hipsters on vacation and city officials at a work conference. One Yelper wrote about the place, "Rock star, starlet, trust fund baby, Stepford wife. It's like they all converge and swim around in that beautiful pool."

Address 601 Eddy Street, San Francisco, CA 94109, +1 415.776.1380, www.jdvhospitality.com | Getting there Bus: 31 (Eddy St & Larkin St stop) | Tip The brunch at Brenda's French Soul Food at 625 Polk Street is a local favorite. On your way there from the Phoenix Hotel, keep your eye out for the five-story mural of a farm girl, painted in muted colors by the artist named Aryz.

83__Pier 24 Photography

A private collection goes public

The piers along the Embarcadero have a long, often moody history. Before the opening of the Bay Bridge in 1936, the wharves served the ferries that linked the city to the East Bay and parts of the Central Valley. Then, during World War II, they were the departure point for soldiers on their way to the Pacific. In 1989, the Loma Prieta earthquake shook down the elevated highway that funneled traffic off Highway 101 to North Beach. The calamity aside, it was a godsend for developers, who for years had been deterred by the way the highway cut the city off from the bay. One venture that abruptly changed the Embarcadero's prospects was the development project known as Mission Rock, organized by the owners of the San Francisco Giants baseball team. Since then, the whole area has had an infusion of investment and renewal.

For 20 years, Pier 24, which has a set of old decaying train tracks that run straight out onto the pier, offered no commercial possibilities. Then a local investment manager named Andrew Pilara appeared on the scene looking for a place to display his impressive photography collection. He instructed his real-estate agent to find him something cheap: "Just a warehouse, nothing fancy." He went on to spend $12 million to transform Pier 24 into the largest exhibition space in the world dedicated solely to photography.

Pier 24 Photography opened in 2010. Separated into a series of exhibition galleries, it shelters the Pilara Foundation Collection, which includes the works of Lee Friedlander, Alfred Stieglitz, Imogen Cunningham, Richard Avedon, Diane Arbus, Dorothea Lange and Robert Mapplethorpe, among many others. It has become one of the city's most important artistic offerings.

There is no entry charge, but you must make an appointment to visit. Only 20 people are admitted per time slot for a quiet and contemplative viewing.

Address Pier 24, The Embarcadero, San Francisco, CA 94105, +1 415.776.1380, www.pier24.org | **Getting there** Light rail: T-Third, N-Judah (Embarcadero & Folsom St stop) | **Hours** By appointment only, +1 415.512.7424 | **Tip** Walk the liveliest part of the San Francisco Bay Trail, which follows the historic State Belt Railroad along the Embarcadero promenade (between Pier 39 and AT&T Park).

84__Pier 70

Industrial ruins with a waterfront view

Once upon a time, beginning in the mid 1800s and lasting for nearly 100 years, the Potrero Point Shipyards comprised the greatest industrial development west of the Mississippi. Located on the southeast shore of the city, it was a hotbed for startup companies of the day: corporations that made steel, ropes, explosives, barrels, rail equipment for streetcars, and mining equipment used to scourge the land-skin off the Gold Country. The air was thick with the smell of forges and the smoke from gas- and ironworks. New ship hulls slid relentlessly down the ramps into the bay: river steamboats and ocean schooners, and Admiral Dewey's flagship, the USS *Olympia*, which later helped blow the Spanish fleet in Manila Bay to smithereens.

The pace of production kept up through World Wars I and II. The final navy ship sailed away in 1965, after which the economy took a downturn and, for the most part, the yards went quiet. One of the very last projects was the making of the underwater tubes used by BART.

Now, little remains of the shipyards, save Pier 70, which has become the symbol of what was – and what may be. The surrounding site, which encompasses more than 60 acres and includes numerous abandoned hangar-like warehouses, industrial workshops, and administrative buildings, has recently become the focus of a massive rebuilding and preservation project. The area is set to include new facilities for artists, museums, and entertaining, plus a good deal of open space. For now, however, one can still wander among the slowly collapsing waterfront ruins. Guided tours of the area are available on the first Sunday of every month.

A bit of trivia for Hitchcock buffs: Pier 70 was one of the settings used in the opening scene of *Vertigo*, where James Stewart meets an old friend, and the "Master of Suspense" makes his signature cameo appearance as one of the passersby.

Address 550 20th Street, San Francisco, CA 94124, pier70sf.org | Getting there Bus: 22, 48 (20th St & 3rd St stop) | Tip RH (formerly Restoration Hardware) moved into the newly renovated Bethlehem Steel Building, with showrooms, an atrium restaurant, and rooftop seating with great views and fire pits.

85_Pink Triangle Park

The only memorial of its kind

In America, the only city to publicly honor gay people imprisoned and killed by the Nazis during World War II is San Francisco. At the intersection of 17th and Market Streets, in the Castro District, you'll find the 3,000-square-foot Pink Triangle Park. It is both somber and strange, but also visually memorable. This small patch of greenery contains 15 triangular stone columns, one for every thousand members of the gay, lesbian, bisexual, and transgender community who perished. The shape of the columns symbolizes the pink triangles sewn on the clothes of "the accused." The sculptures were created by local artists Susan Martin and Robert Bruce. Each five-foot-tall pylon is composed of Sierra granite.

The park was dedicated in 2001 by a local neighborhood association that wanted to establish "a physical reminder of how the persecution of any individual or single group of people damages all humanity." It has become a signature landmark of the Castro, which became a gay district in the 1970s. It was during World War II that San Francisco saw a significant increase to its gay population, following the dishonorable discharge of thousands of servicemen bound for the Pacific.

Between 1933 and 1945, an estimated 100,000 gay men were arrested throughout Germany and Austria on charges of homosexuality. Half of those were prosecuted; and of that number between 5,000 and 15,000 were dispatched to concentration camps. This atrocity was often unacknowledged in any country after the war, but in 2002 the German government publicly apologized to the gay community.

Once a year, during the San Francisco Pride weekend in June, a one-acre pink triangle made up of dozens of pieces of blush-colored canvas unfolds on the north side of the Twin Peaks, proudly facing the Castro district and downtown San Francisco.

Address Market Street & 17th Street, San Francisco, CA 94114, pinktrianglepark.org | Getting there Streetcar: F-Line (17th St & Castro St stop) | Tip Another solemn spot that offers a chance for reflection and remembrance is the National AIDS Memorial Grove in Golden Gate Park on Bowling Green Drive.

86 Point Bonita Lighthouse

Overlooking an underwater graveyard

Hundreds of ships have been wrecked on the rocks and beaches around San Francisco Bay; many during the Gold Rush in the 1850s. Some ships foundered around Fort Point, which is underneath what is now the southern end of the Golden Gate Bridge. Others were thrown up on Ocean Beach. The most famous of those, in 1878, was the *King Philip*, a three-masted clipper ship, the skeleton of whose hull is still visible occasionally.

Long before this, however, the carnage had already led to the building of a brick-and-concrete lighthouse at Point Bonita on the Marin Headlands, in 1855. The tower stood 306 feet above the ocean. The problem was that the light wasn't visible to approaching ships because fog along the West Coast of the United States, unlike the East Coast, settles at a higher altitude. In 1877, the lighthouse was relocated to another site just 124 feet above sea level.

And still there were wrecks. On the morning of February 22, 1901, the iron-hulled, steam-powered passenger liner, the SS *City of Rio de Janeiro* hit a reef close to Fort Point. The ship, filled with Asian emigrants – and American crew members who couldn't speak Chinese – was returning from Hong Kong. The ship sank in just twenty minutes. A court finding later noted, "The fog was so dense that the day afforded no light. It was very dark, but the water was smooth." Of the 210 people on board, 82 survived. In July 1902, the ship's pilothouse washed up on Baker Beach. Inside was the partly decomposed body of the captain, William Ward, who had once vowed he would go down with his ship.

To reach the lighthouse, drive along the road that winds up the Marin Headlands until you reach the trailhead. A short, steep pathway leads down to a hand-carved tunnel framed in bright red ironized stone. A suspension footbridge carries you above the furious waves to the lighthouse, whose light can be seen from 18 miles away.

Address Point Bonita Trailhead, Field Road, Sausalito, CA 94965, www.nps.gov/goga/pobo.htm | **Getting there** Bus: 76X (Field Rd & Light House stop) | **Hours** Sat–Mon 12:30–3:30pm | **Tip** Wear good walking shoes and many layers of clothing to protect yourself from the cold winds.

87 Portals of the Past

A bit of history and the occult on Lloyd Lake

Among the wild animals living in Golden Gate Park, besides corralled buffalo, are feral cats, raccoons, and two or three coyotes that appear and disappear like phantoms, often at sunup or sunset. If you happen to catch sight of them, don't be surprised if they look you right in the eye before moving on, like fugitives on the run – but a slow, casual, Butch Cassidy kind of run. The message is: "This is our territory, and we reserve the right to go after small dogs and other prey you may have with you." And they do.

There are all kinds of birds in the park. Occasionally, you may see store-bought birds that have flown the coop, or various species of duck. At Lloyd Lake, for example, between JFK Drive and Crossover Drive, you'll see Pekin ducks (aka Long Island ducks), Muscovy ducks (bred from pre-Columbian times and native to Mexico), Campbell ducks (the khaki-suited characters originally from England), mallards, and geese.

Lloyd Lake is also interesting for other reasons, including the marble portico standing on its shore, which originally came from the Nob Hill home of Alban Nelson Towne. Towne was a 19th-century railroad man, a clever and respected technocrat, who acquired a small fortune. The portico is all that was left after the 1906 earthquake destroyed his home. Three years later, Towne's wife donated the structure to the park, where it's become known as "Portals of the Past." On a cold, foggy afternoon it looks like something out of Henry James's *The Turn of the Screw*.

Actually, the portico is one of a few locales in the park where occult "sightings" have been rumored. Also called the Shadowbox, it was a favorite haunt of early-20th-century spiritualists, including the likes of Arthur Conan Doyle, who in 1923 imagined the setting as "a place that opens the receptive soul to dangerous influences. It should not be visited carelessly."

Address John F. Kennedy Drive & 23rd Avenue, San Francisco, CA 94121, www.golden-gate-park.com/lloyd-lake.html | Getting there Bus: 29 (Cross Over Dr & Fulton St stop) | Tip John F. Kennedy Drive is closed to cars on Sundays, making it the perfect time to take a bike ride along the seven miles of paved trails leading you by lush waterfalls and gardens. Equipment can be rented at Stow Lake Bike & Boat Rentals (50 Stow Lake Drive, +1 415.752.0347).

88 The Presidio Pet Cemetery

Final resting place for the furry and feathered

The gravestones include such names as Heidi, Willie, Trouble, and Mr. Iguana. Heidi was a ten-year-old collie. Willie was a hamster. Trouble was nine years of "no trouble," but what species we'll never know. And Mr. Iguana? It seems the name speaks for itself.

These are just a few of the hundreds of interred animals in the city's most notable pet cemetery, which you'll find in the Presidio, directly under the new and "reimagined" Doyle Drive, that looming viaduct leading to and from the Golden Gate Bridge. In the last few years the causeway has been seismically retrofitted, and these days the pet cemetery is best seen in passing. Entry is forbidden – at least until the highway reconstruction is complete, no later than 2016.

The cemetery grounds, about the size of a small soccer field, have long been neglected and left to ruin. At one time, it was all quite elaborate and treasured, but now many of the gravestones have cracked or collapsed. The dilapidated white picket fence is no longer white and is made redundant by a chain-link enclosure. Even the jade plants have turned black. Only two palm trees enliven the landscape.

Still, the fading headstones provide endearing tidbits about the beloved pets buried there, most of whom came from military families in the 1950s and 1960s. There is the stone that simply reads, "Sarge," and another that's inscribed, "A G.I. Pet, he did his time." There's the parakeet referred to as "Our Knucklehead," and the dog named "Sheesa-nut."

On one grave, the epitaph states, "George accepted us people." There are some stones with big red hearts to mark the unknown. And then there's the grave of "Bali Boring," a toy poodle belonging to "Major and Mrs. Boring."

The cemetery is also home to at least one living feline resident – a black cat, clearly feral, itching and licking, and no doubt content in this gopher heaven.

Address 667 McDowell Avenue, San Francisco, CA 94129, www.presidio.gov/explore/Pages/presidio-pet-cemetery.aspx | **Getting there** Bus: 28 (Golden Gate Br Tunnel & Merchant Rd stop) | **Tip** Take a walk down to historic Fort Point to learn more about this incredible former military site and enjoy a great view of the Golden Gate Bridge.

89 Project Artaud

The artist factory

Despite San Francisco's reputation as a haven for the creative classes, the artists that have flocked here always seem hard-pressed to find affordable housing amidst the ever-skyrocketing real-estate market. But innovation is often desperation's child, and one of the best examples of this is Project Artaud, the city's first live-work space for artists. It was established in 1971 and named after mid-20th-century French surrealist playwright and poet Antonin Artaud, who famously said, "No one has ever written, painted, sculpted, modeled, built, or invented except literally to get out of hell."

Project Artaud is set up in the old American Can Company factory and spans an entire block on the edge of the Mission District. Working as carpenters and builders themselves to renovate the building, the artists who moved in embodied the idea of collectively seizing control of artistic production and presentation. Since then, their work has become the bedrock of the city's avant-garde cultural life.

Today, Project Artaud is home and hive to some 80 artists, including musicians, writers, sculptors, dancers, a robot designer, and a vaudevillian. The building also includes several performance spaces, such as the Theatre of Yugen, whose ensemble explores traditional Japanese aesthetics, and Z Space, one of the local incubators for new theatrical works. The Z Space Gallery, which displays a changing selection of works (often by resident artists) is open during the day, and is a great way to visit the complex. Along 17th Street you can also see the delightful umbrellas sculpture by artist Benjy Young.

Most evenings at Project Artaud, there are performances of some kind, be it dance, comedy, drama, or music. One unique and not-to-be-missed theater group is Word for Word, which stages productions of classic and contemporary fiction, read aloud, literally verbatim.

Address 499 Alabama Street, San Francisco, CA 94110, +1 415.621.4240, www.projectartaud.org | Getting there Bus: 12 (Folsom St & 18th St stop) | Hours Visit the website for performance schedules, gallery hours, and Open Studios information | Tip Several times a year Project Artaud hosts Open Studios, during which the public can wander through the artists' creative spaces. While you're in the area, take a walk to 3057 17th Street, where you'll find the nostalgic old Police Station, built in 1899 in the Romanesque Revival style.

90_The Ramp

Fog City's hangover cure

For decades the Ramp was a true hidden Dogpatch gem – an out-of-the-way waterfront dive with an irresistible charm and sense of history. It was just as the poet Ralph Gutlohn said: "It's such a relief to see something that's not fixed up in this city, that's just left the way it is."

It was the kind of place you could surprise someone for a private afternoon date: "I'll take you somewhere I'll bet you've never been – and by the way, you can bring your dog!" And then you'd zip down Third Street to China Basin, and over average food, you'd sit together outside at a lacquered table, feeling the saltwater breeze, with the pelicans and the boats on the bay in the background.

The Ramp opened in 1950 and started out as no more than a bait shop. It expanded to include a bar offering no-frills snacks, and eventually became a casual dockside restaurant. And, of course, there was always the nearby ramp, from which anyone could launch their boat into the bay. Patrons included sailors, sanders, fitters, and electricians – all the tradespeople readying boats for trial.

In the 1980s, Donald K. White, a local business writer, penned a regular newspaper column about lunch with two invented characters, George and Adele, and their French poodle, Sir. It was a conceit to educate people about the stock market. Often, White's fictional meals took place at the Ramp.

In the nineties, the bar became more widely known, and most recently it was the backdrop for a comical double-date scene in the 2013 Woody Allen movie Blue Jasmine, starring Cate Blanchett.

Perhaps not quite the well-guarded secret it once was, the Ramp remains a favorite haunt among San Franciscans and is far off the beaten tourist path. The Sunday brunch is known locally as a tried and true hangover cure, and the classic order is a Bloody Mary or Ramos Fizz with either Huevos Rancheros or Eggs Benny.

Address 855 Terry A. Francois Boulevard, San Francisco, CA 94158, +1 415.621.2378, www.therampresturant.com | Getting there Light rail: T-Third (3rd St & Mariposa St stop) | Hours Daily 10am–9pm | Tip The Ramp offers live salsa music and dancing every Saturday or Sunday afternoon from May to October.

91 The Rock Colony

Where music legends lived and "free loved"

A fluke in city planning helped create the counterculture mecca that was Haight-Ashbury in the 1960s. Many of the grand old Victorian houses, like the pink wedding-cake affair at 635 Ashbury, where Janis Joplin lived, had been subdivided for workers during WW II. When the workers moved in during the 1950s, the city drafted plans to run a freeway along the Panhandle. Real-estate values in the area plummeted, rents decreased, and then, as now, the artists followed.

The freeway never came, but the musicians did, creating a unique rock style – a blend of the improvisational spirit of jazz with psychedelic imagery and folk melodies – that came to be known as the San Francisco Sound. Many of its legendary artists resided in the Haight-Ashbury neighborhood at various times.

The side of the building where Jimi Hendrix once lived, 1524 Haight Street, sports a mural of him playing his guitar, and the funky curtains in the window suggest that bohemia still keeps a toehold here. Nothing so wild can be found at 710 Ashbury, where the Grateful Dead hung out in the late sixties. The big house is now decidedly buttoned down; no Jerry in a top hat on the front porch, no girls climbing out the window. The dark brown exterior seems to banish any rainbow-tie-dye dreams that might still linger in the woodwork.

Somehow Jefferson Airplane's house at 2400 Fulton remains most like the music of the band that lived there. The giant Greek Revival mansion with oversized columns would be the perfect place to live if you were "Alice when you're ten feet tall." The band members resided in the mansion's 17 rooms at the height of their fame in '68 and '69. The exterior was painted pure black then and the parties they hosted were legendary. The stature of the "Airplane house" is also a reminder of the profits that the music counterculture brought to San Francisco; as Grace Slick later sang, "We built this city on rock and roll."

Address 635 Ashbury Street (Janice Joplin), 1524 Haight Street (Jimi Hendrix), 2400 Fulton Street (Jefferson Airplane), San Francisco, CA 94117 | Getting there Bus: 33 (Ashbury St & Haight St stop); 6, 71 (Haight St & Masonic Ave stop); 5 (Fulton St & Arguello Blvd stop) | Tip Check out Mendel's Far Out Fabrics and Art Supplies at 1556 Haight Street, where you can pick up materials to make your own rock star outfit.

92_The Rousseaus

One man, many facades

Inland from Ocean Beach lies the Outer Sunset District, once a vast sand tundra known as the "Outside Lands." In the late 19th century, it became a less-forbidding beach bohemia. Over the next hundred years it evolved into a middle-class neighborhood, home to various immigrant groups, including Germans and Irish, and most recently, Chinese.

Architectural signatures in the Outer Sunset include horse-drawn streetcars that were transformed into getaway houses in 1895, earthquake shacks built after the earthquake of 1906, and the affordable housing units built by Henry Doelger in the 1920s and 1930s. But there's one other defining architectural oddity worth noting: along 34th, 35th, and 36th Avenues between Kirkham and Lawton Streets, you'll find a potpourri of idiosyncratic houses reminiscent of something you might see on a film-studio back lot. The houses, known as Rousseaus, were built by Oliver Rousseau, on whose death, in 1977, San Francisco's most prominent chronicler, Herb Caen, noted, "Another Memorial Day death: Oliver Rousseau, who built good houses while all about him, the pure schlock was rising."

These "good houses" are slightly bigger than Doelger's and more upscale in every way. Today they sell for $1 million or more. Each shows a different facade; some with a turret, others with a Moorish arch or a full-length second-story balcony. There are houses with mansard roofs and houses with red-tiled Spanish roofs. Some are gingerbread-like, others are in the Tudor, Mediterranean, or Parisian style. Ornamental details – such as glazed tiles, entryway medallions, finials, and ironwork – vary from house to house.

Inside, the atmospheres are equally whimsical. Designs include sunken living rooms, interior gardens, and tiled bathrooms in bold unusual color combinations. It's all faux and fantastic, theme-less and timeless, incongruent but interesting.

Address 34th, 35th & 36th Avenues, between Kirkham and Lawton Streets, San Francisco, CA 94122 | Getting there Light rail: N-Judah (Judah St & 34th Ave stop) | Tip The Rousseau houses are an easy detour on your way to Ocean Beach or Golden Gate Park.

93_Saint John Coltrane African Orthodox Church

Worship in the house of jazz

Among the city's vertebrae is Fillmore Street, which was named after America's 13th president, Millard Fillmore, a member of the Whig party and a free marketeer, who was also antislavery, anti-immigration, and anti-manifest destiny. His idiosyncratic platform matches San Francisco's character to a tee.

Fillmore is best known for its music scene, a reputation that's epitomized by the legendary Fillmore Auditorium, which has hosted a range of iconic bands over the decades from the Grateful Dead to Radiohead. The street was also once the city's Holy Land of jazz, even before World War I, and today the most popular jazz venues can still be found here, including Yoshi's and the Boom Boom Room.

Just a short block from Yoshi's, behind a tinted storefront window, is Saint John Coltrane African Orthodox Church. Every Sunday morning the front door opens to the small space, decorated with murals of a black Mary and Jesus, and of the congregation's unique patron saint, John Coltrane. In one large painting by Reverend Mark Dukes, a golden halo encircles Coltrane's head, as he holds a scripture in one hand and a flaming tenor saxophone in the other.

The first tip-off that this isn't your average Sunday service is the electric keyboard, drum kit, and two basses set up next to the altar. The weekly ritual begins with one hour of incense-filled meditation, listening to the album, A Love Supreme. Two hours of liturgy follows, during which the music of the jazz giant is played with passion and joy by the church's band and anyone who wants to join the jam session (all attending are welcome to bring their own instruments).

The church was founded in 1969 by archbishop Franzo Wayne King and Reverend Mother Marina King, who saw Coltrane perform in 1965, and immediately felt the "presence of God" in his music.

Address Fort Mason Center for Arts & Culture, 2 Marina Boulevard, San Francisco, CA 94123, +1.415.673.7144, www.coltranechurch.org | **Getting there** Bus: 28, 28L (Marina Blvd stop) | **Hours** Sunday service 11am–1pm | **Tip** Next door is the Italo-Americano Museum, celebrating Italian history and artists with Italian roots (www.sfmuseo.org).

94 Saints Peter and Paul Church

Home base of a neighborhood

In North Beach, along the edge of Washington Square, stands Saints Peter and Paul Church. Notable for its twin towers, it was built in 1912 as an outpost for the Salesians, of the Society of Saint Francis de Sales, founded by Saint John Bosco in the 19th century. Bosco's motto was "Give me souls, you can have the rest."

The "rest" were the hearts and minds of immigrants who made their way across America and gave North Beach neighborhoods their Italian identities. At the center of these communities has always been Saints Peter and Paul, which includes a school but is perhaps best known for its Salesian Boys' and Girls' Club. The club has always attracted the children of the city's great Italian families, and also has a cherished reputation for its sports teams, particularly baseball.

Among the church's early parishioners was a Sicilian fisherman and his wife, the DiMaggios, whose son Joe could hit baseballs to the moon. He would go on to become the "Yankee Clipper" – one of the greatest players who ever lived. In 1939, he married his first wife, Dorothy Arnold, at the church. She was the sultry-eyed heroine of the B-movie classic The Phantom Creeps. They divorced in 1944.

Joe's second wife was Hollywood bombshell Marilyn Monroe. By one account DiMaggio had hoped to wed Monroe at Saints Peter and Paul but was denied by Catholic doctrine. After their civil ceremony they returned to the church's steps to take photos as newlyweds. Years later, in 1999, DiMaggio's funeral was held there.

The turn-of-the-century church was also a setting in Richard Brautigan's 1967 novel *Trout Fishing in America*, and in the 1971 movie *Dirty Harry*, with Clint Eastwood. On the first Sunday of October, a procession from Saints Peter and Paul to the Fisherman's Wharf celebrates an old Sicilian tradition: the Blessing of the Fishing Fleet.

Address 666 Filbert Street, San Francisco, CA 94133, www.salesiansspp.org | Getting there Bus: 8X, 41, 45 (Columbus Ave & Union St stop); 30 (Columbus Ave & Filbert St stop) Hours Mon–Fri 7am–4pm, Sat & Sun 7am–6pm | Tip A warm green onion focaccia sandwich is a must at Mario Bohemian Cigar Store Café, just across the park on the corner of Union and Green Streets.

95 Sam's Grill

A historic chophouse with a fishy past

Sam's is one of the old staples in the financial district, an out-of-the-way "in" joint for brokers, agents, publishers and financiers – primarily men – who have just enough time for a an oyster cocktail, a minute steak, and a tiramisu. The menu claims this is the fifth-oldest restaurant in the country. There's no sawdust on the floor, but there might as well be; Sam's is an old-fashioned chophouse with dark wooden booths and waiters in black tie with white napkins hanging from their forearms like fresh laundry. They're mostly gray-haired men, much like the customers, dashing up and down the floors with Sam's signature dishes, petrale and rex sole, and sand crabs.

Sam's is on the corner of Bush Street and Belden Place. It opened in 1867 at the will of an Irish native named Michael Bolan Moraghan, who started a huge oyster farm in the South Bay, in an area the size of San Francisco. In 1900 the farm was giving up more than 2.5 million pounds of oyster meat a year. And that despite the likes of Jack London and other so-called oyster pirates. Now the beds are long gone – largely because of pollution, weather extremes, and – some would add bitterly – government regulation.

The restaurant got its name from Sam Zenovich, a restaurateur who bought Moraghan's in 1922 and filled the place with such sports celebrities as heavyweight boxing champs John L. Sullivan, James J. Corbett, and Jack Dempsey. Sam died in 1937 and the restaurant has been passed from owner to owner ever since. The menu still includes oysters but they have become increasingly harder to farm profitably as land-use battles between those who want to create new marine sanctuaries on public land and those who want to hold on to commercial opportunities have slowed down supply. It's one more example of how the balance between population and resources is reaching a tipping point throughout the Bay Area.

Address 374 Bush Street, San Francisco, CA 94104, +1 415.421.0594, www.samsgrill-sf.com | **Getting there** Bus: 1 (Clay St & Kearny St stop); 38 AX (Bush St & Sansome St stop) | **Hours** Mon–Fri 11am–8:30pm | **Tip** Walk down to Union Square to check out the four painted heart sculptures from the Hearts in San Francisco public art installation, located at each of the four corners of the square.

96 San Francisco Art Institute

All hail Diego Rivera

One of the city's points of cultural pride is the San Francisco Art Institute, which was founded in 1871 by artists and writers trying to create something entirely new, a critical mass of artistic expression that would define a distinctly Western point of view.

Among the early artists associated with the school was Eadweard Muybridge, the great photographer whose famous motion studies of horses was pivotal in the advancement of cinematography; the Western impressionist (and poet) Maynard Dixon, who, incidentally, contributed to the murals in the Mark Hopkins Hotel; Louise Dahl-Wolfe, who developed the notion of "environmental" fashion photography; and, of course, the great muralist Diego Rivera, some of whose iconic work remains in the institute's collection and is on permanent exhibition in the student-directed gallery space.

Following World War II, the school, which is at 800 Chestnut Street, became a center for Abstract Expressionism. The faculty included the likes of Clyfford Still, Ad Reinhardt, Mark Rothko, David Park, and Elmer Bischoff. Ansel Adams cofounded the photography department.

Since 1961, the institute has sought to merge the notions of fine and applied arts and become a breeding ground for many forms of creative expression, including punk music, graffiti art, and more recently, community art projects. The institute offers various degree programs through its School of Studio Practice and School of Interdisciplinary Studies.

Located on Russian Hill, the building that houses the institute is a Spanish-style structure, complete with a bell tower. A visit up to the rooftop delivers a breathtaking experience. There are few other places in San Francisco that provide such a sweeping view of the city's rolling hills and the bay. The panoramic vista spans east to west, from the Embarcadero and Coit Tower to Pier 39 and Alcatraz.

Address 800 Chestnut Street, San Francisco, CA 94133, +1 415.771.7020, www.sfai.edu | **Getting there** Bus: 30 (Chestnut St & Van Ness Ave stop) | **Hours** Daily 9am–6pm | **Tip** Take a short walk to the hidden petite Fay Park at 2366 Leavenworth Street. Enjoy the serenity and the shade offered by the two gazebos in this public parklet. There is a wonderful sundial with the inscription: "Grow old along with me, the best is yet to be."

97_SoundBox

The new cachet of classical music

The tired trope in the performing arts this day, particularly for big city symphonies, is that the audience is graying and dying off. Plus, the whole experience of sitting trapped in your seat for 90 minutes, unable even to text and post, is the new-new, bad-bad, near-death experience. The local story is that the median age in San Francisco is 39, but the median age of San Francisco Symphony patrons is 64. As an aside, the influence of Silicon Valley wealth has begun to affect philanthropic streams so that donors expect beneficiaries like the symphony to perform more like start-ups. This thinking extends to audience development. As one symphony CEO put it, "Funders want results!"

So the new business strategy is to downsize and localize the classical music concert experience, create satellite spaces, incorporate multimedia, mix musical genres, highlight solo instruments and musicians, and create a cabaret atmosphere, with food and alcohol. And cell phones. Trust people to "self-regulate" their use of phones. Don't expect full engagement. And don't ever begin a concert with an admonishment. Think in terms of an audience under 40 that will turn trendy into cachet.

In San Francisco, the symphony decided to work with these new norms. It has been experimenting since 2014 with a club-like venue called SoundBox, an "industrial cavern" under Davies Symphony Hall. It's all a new kind of "social experience," where one is able to sit six feet away from a master cellist performing a Bach suite. The programming at SoundBox includes traditional classical music and the avant-garde. From Monteverdi to Cage, to Ligeti to Samuel Adams. The mantra at SoundBox is. "No guidelines. We just tell people where the exits are and then go for it." The space is augmented with a state-of-the-art Meyer Constellation Sound System. Seating is limited, so many in the audience stand.

Address 300 Franklin Street, San Francisco, CA 94102, +1 415.503.5299, www.sfsoundbox.com, info@sfsoundbox.com | **Getting there** Light rail: M-Ocean View (Van Ness stop) | **Hours** Check the website for the performance schedule. | **Tip** San Francisco classic restaurant Zuni at 1658 Market Street, San Francisco CA 94102, www.zunicafe.com is perfect for a dinner before or after the performance.

98_Stow Lake

The ghost of the White Lady

Naturally, San Francisco has its urban legends. Underneath the Palace of the Legion of Honor, for example, a cemetery established during the Gold Rush gave rise to a story that when it came time to move the graveyard in order to make room for the palace, grave diggers quickly tired of the task and simply carried away the headstones, leaving some 11,000 bodies in the ground. The spirits, it is said, have never departed.

And then there's the ghost of 18-year-old Flora Sommerton, sometimes seen on Nob Hill, along California Street between Jones and Powell. In 1876, her parents arranged her marriage to a much older man, which prompted Flora to run away to Butte, Montana, where her body was found years later in a flophouse – still clad in the ball gown she'd been wearing when she disappeared. She appeared to have been living in terrible poverty at the time of her death. If you see her, she's still trying to get home; don't get in her way.

Of all the city's legends, the most heartbreaking is the White Lady of Stow Lake, where lovers and families row boats in the midst of Golden Gate Park, just west of the Japanese Tea Garden. The story goes that more than a century ago, a mother sat down next to the lake on a park bench, with her child in a stroller. The mother fell into a conversation with a stranger and didn't notice the stroller slowly rolling into the water. When the conversation ended the lady realized her child was missing and ran screaming through the park asking people, "Have you seen my baby?" She searched all day and night and finally thought of the lake. She was last seen wading into the water near the bench.

That bereft mother is still occasionally seen coming out of the lake, always at dusk, dressed in white, her hair sopping wet, desperately asking people, "Have you seen my baby?" If you say yes, she will haunt you; if you say no, she will kill you.

Address 50 Stow Lake Drive, San Francisco, CA 94118, www.stowlakeboathouse.com | Getting there Bus: 28, 29 (19th Ave & Lincoln Way stop) | Tip Strawberry Hill is the naturally formed island in the middle of Stow Lake and affords great views of the surrounding park, the Golden Gate Bridge, and Mount Tamalpais. Access the island from one of two bridges and enjoy a nice hike through lush foliage and past an artificial waterfall.

99__Sutro Heights Park

A garden of earthly delight

What a grand place it once was, millionaire Adolph Sutro's vision of an earthly paradise. His house and grounds overlooked the ocean, along with baths, a concert hall, a museum, a skating rink, and the Cliff House. And now, it's all ruins.

But at the end of the 19th century, coming across the outer lands from distant downtown, visitors arrived at a real-life fantasy landscape. Sutro spent more than $1 million to recreate an elaborate and intricate Italian garden on the 22-acre site, embellishing it with 200 replicas of Greek statues and urns placed among exotic plants and trees, all of which was open to the public.

Sutro, who served as San Francisco's mayor from 1894 to 1896, hosted presidents, writers, artists and the celebrities of the day – from Andrew Carnegie to Oscar Wilde – at his estate. You can almost imagine Wilde arriving in San Francisco in 1882 to give his famous lecture, "The House Beautiful," and strolling through Sutro's gardens afterward, perhaps envisioning what it would be like to give up London and come west, "where a man can be a man today, and yesterdays don't count." The five days he spent in San Francisco made a particular impression on Wilde, later expressed in *The Picture of Dorian Gray*, when Lord Henry notes: "It's an odd thing, but anyone who disappears is said to be seen in San Francisco."

Following Sutro's death in 1898, the property slowly fell into disrepair and was finally demolished after his family donated the land, the gardens, and their home as a public recreation area to the city in 1938. Practically the only reminders of Sutro's shangri-la today are replicas of the winged lions guarding the entry to what once was. To visitors who don't wonder at the ramparts or inquire as to the origins of the park's name, it's just a lovely picnic area with a view of the Farallon Islands in the distance – and in the foreground, a few statues and a gazebo.

Address 48th Avenue & Point Lobos Avenue, San Francisco, CA 94121 | **Getting there** Bus: 38 (43rd Ave & Point Lobos Ave stop) | **Tip** You can spend the night across the street at Seal Rock Inn (545 Point Lobos Avenue), where Hunter S. Thompson stayed in the early seventies.

100 Swedenborgian Church

Sacred space hidden in plain sight

Emanuel Swedenborg was the 18th-century rationalist who believed in angels. At 53, he had a series of spiritual encounters that led to his most famous work, *Heaven and Hell*, in which he described angels this way: "They have faces, eyes, ears, chests, arms, hands, and feet. They see each other, hear each other, and talk to each other. In short, they lack nothing that belongs to humans except that they are not clothed with a material body."

Swedenborg was a scientist and inventor as well as a psychic and Christian mystic, and influenced the likes of Ralph Waldo Emerson, William Blake, Carl Jung, and Helen Keller. Swedenborg was never interested in founding a church, but after his death, in 1772, reading groups devoted to his work sprang up and spread to America, where several churches were built in the 1800s.

In 1895, a Swedenborgian church was constructed in San Francisco in the heart of Pacific Heights. The great American poet Robert Frost regularly attended the Swedenborgian Church Sunday School as a youth. "I know San Francisco like my own face," Frost said late in his life. "It's where I came from, the first place I really knew. You always know where you come from, don't you?"

The church, surrounded by a high wall, has the most lovely garden, which includes various trees chosen for their symbolic value: a redwood tree, an olive tree, a Japanese maple, a Lebanese cedar, an Irish yew. It all has less the look of a church than perhaps a meditation center or urban monastery. It's one of the earliest examples of the Arts and Crafts movement in San Francisco. The architect was A. Page Brown; the draftsman, Bernard Maybeck. The design was influenced by painter William Keith, who did several of the murals inside, and the naturalist John Muir. The roof is made from reddish madrones from the Santa Cruz mountains. The gate is usually open to view the garden.

Address 2107 Lyon Street, San Francisco, CA 94115, +1 415.346.6466, www.sfswedenborgian.org | Getting there Bus: 1 (California St & Baker St stop) | Hours Mon–Fri 10am–6pm | Tip At 2300 Fillmore Street, Nest is a charming little store offering French bohemian gifts and home decor.

101__The Taj Mahal

Boats by any other name

In the houseboat culture of the Bay Area, the two most famous landmarks include one boat dressed up like the Taj Mahal and the other like a small Gilligan's Island. Both were made in a Sausalito dockyard by an eccentric millionaire named Forbes Thor Kiddoo. He was a carpenter from Brooklyn who became a wharf rat in Marin, where he started a wildly successful company that turned out homes built on barges. Houseboats were all the rage in Sausalito in the late 1960s and early 1970s, and Kiddoo developed new building techniques and designs. His company built more than one 100 houseboats before it was forced to close in 1986 due to local restrictions.

It took five years and about a million dollars to build his 50-by-100-foot, 700-ton "island," which was launched in 1980. The original design included three staterooms, all with private baths, and a waterfall that flowed into a hot tub. It had finely crafted doors made without nails and portholes taken from famous ships, as well as tons of rock and sand and enough topsoil to grow towering palm trees – all surrounded by a white picket fence. But the piece de resistance was a 40-foot-tall lighthouse. The floating estate was featured on *Lifestyles of the Rich and Famous*, and appeared around the bay until 1990, when Kiddoo transformed it into a restaurant that is now moored at Pier 39 along the Embarcadero.

His other creation, the *Taj Mahal*, lives in Richardson Bay, and was roughly inspired by the original building after which it was named. Altogether, it's a waterfront folly of arabesques, ogee arches, cupolas, colonnades, and fiberglass domes. It was completed in the 1970s as a three-level, 4,500-square-foot home with such accouterments as a sauna, spa, and heated tile floor. Sadly, the houseboat was badly damaged in a March 2023 "bomb cyclone." It has been stabilized, and future plans for it are emerging.

Address Taj Mahal, Pier at Johnson Street, Sausalito, CA 94965 | Getting there From the San Francisco Ferry Building take the Sausalito Ferry to Sausalito, walk a few blocks north to the last pier at Johnson Street. | Hours Not open to the public, viewable from the pier only | Tip In Sausalito, you can enjoy a nice walk around Schoonmaker Point and a delicious lunch at the French restaurant Le Garage.

102_Tenderloin National Forest

A quiet sliver of green amid the chaos

The Tenderloin District is the city's "gut"; a gritty 50-block area roughly bordered by Geary Boulevard and Union Square to the north, the Civic Center to the south, Market Street to the east, and City Hall to the west. Its name refers to a similar neighborhood in late-19th-century New York City, and it has been popularized in such books as Dashiell Hammett's *The Maltese Falcon*.

Although in recent years the incidence of violence in the Tenderloin has receded, the district is still known locally for corpses, as well as live nude girls, suburban johns, transvestites, gang members, big-time jazz musicians (the likes of Brubeck and Monk), writers, actors, felons and ex cons, refugees from Vietnam and the Philippines, Palestinians running the corner markets, and of course transients down on their luck – or their mental health.

And in the midst of this urban wilderness is the "Tenderloin National Forest," formally known as Cohen Alley, a 25 by 136-foot strip of green space between Hyde and Leavenworth Streets. At the entrance you'll find a massive handcrafted wrought-iron gate that's generally open from 10am to 5pm beyond which is a unique interlude of lush foliage, trees, boxes of herbs and edible flowers, and a fish pond surrounded by bright murals and a mosaic-covered floor.

Artists Darryl Smith and Laurie Lazer of the Luggage Store Gallery have been slowly transforming the alley into this little art oasis since 1989. It's a quiet and peaceful sanctuary nestled in a cluster of residential buildings and hotels, an eccentric gathering spot to enjoy public art – and the right place to come if you need your slacks mended or a button replaced: on the 15th of every month, the artist Michael Swaine arrives with his old sewing machine and repairs clothing free of charge.

Address 509 Ellis Street, San Francisco, CA 94109, +1 415.255.5971, www.luggagestoregallery.org | **Getting there** Bus: 38 (O'Farrell St & Leavenworth St stop) | **Hours** Tue–Fri 11am–3pm | **Tip** Stop in for an inexpensive and tasty banh mi at Saigon Sandwich (560 Larkin), which the *New York Times* has said "may be the best in America."

103 Tessie Wall Townhouse

Home of a trigger-happy madam

Among the prominent madams of the Barbary Coast, as the city's former red-light district was known in the 19th century, was Ah Toy, a beautiful and expensive Chinese courtesan. She was intelligent and direct – and ran a slave trade. Then there was Mary Ellen Pleasant, an African-American woman known as the Voodoo Queen, who operated a cathouse, married a wealthy banker, and became one of America's first civil rights crusaders.

Another infamous madam was "Belle," who was the mistress of a local gambler, Charles Cora. One night in 1855, he took her to the theater, and sitting in front of them was a U.S. marshal who pronounced Belle's presence offensive. Cora refused to leave and three days later shot the marshal dead. A trial resulted in a hung jury, which caused an uproar fueled by a yellow journalist named James King. When King was murdered by a local politician, the notorious Committee of Vigilance of 1856 was created to restore justice. Their first act was to hang both King's killer and Cora, who married Belle in jail shortly before being executed.

But the most legendary and successful madam of the period was Tessie Wall (1869–1932), an Irish-Catholic girl with blue eyes, blond hair, and an ironic smile, who could drink a man under the table. Her first husband, a fireman, died, leaving her with a child and no money. Eventually, she opened a high-class bordello and married a political boss named Frank Daroux. Their home was at 535 Powell Street, a three-story mansion that Tessie filled with the expensive antique furnishings she was known to collect. When Daroux ordered her to quit her extremely lucrative business she refused. He filed for divorce and took up with another woman; she shot him, three times. He survived, but declined to press charges; she got off scot-free. When the cops asked Tessie why she did it, she's said to have replied, "I shot him 'cause I love him, damn him!"

Address 535 Powell St, San Francisco, CA 94108 | **Getting there** Cable car: Powell/Mason, Powell/Hyde (Powell St & Sutter St stop) | **Tip** If you're in the mood for theater, try the TIX half-price ticket booth on Union Square plaza. They sell same-day tickets to plays and shows in the nearby theater district.

104 Tin How Temple

The How of Tao

Grant Avenue is the tourist route through the city's fabled Chinatown, but layers of ancient Asian culture are still hidden here in the smaller streets and alleyways. When Chinese immigrants first made the voyage to "Gold Mountain," the Chinese name for California during the Gold Rush, one of their first missions was to thank the deity who guided them safely across the Pacific. The temple they built to honor the goddess Tin How (also known as Mazu) in 1852 is still in its original location, and is the oldest Taoist temple in America.

Tin How was a legendary woman of 9th-century coastal China. With her preternatural skills as a swimmer and sailor, she saved many a drowning seafarer, to become a sort of patron saint of those making sea voyages, and remains widely worshipped to this day.

This knowledge may or may not help you sort out the hundreds of statues and images that await you at the top of three flights of very steep, creaky wooden steps in the Tin How Temple. Don't worry that the door of the narrow building is unmarked or that there are no signs, or that the permanently grumpy person who may or may not be in the shrine room will almost certainly not speak English. This is a public space; people come here to pray, and as long as you are respectful and quiet you will be tolerated, though photos are strictly forbidden.

The elaborately carved red-and-gold shrine room glows with lantern light and candles, its air dense with clouds of incense. Red paper banners hang like stalactites from the ceiling, bearing the Chinese names of the many supplicants who come here to ask a blessing or a favor. It's a good idea to leave a donation, for the goddess of your choice. And don't miss the view of Waverly Place from the fire escape/terrace out front. From this angle, 19th-century China appears to be right before your eyes.

Address 125 Waverly Plaza, San Francisco, CA 94108 | **Getting there** Bus: 1 (Clay St & Stockton St stop) | **Hours** Daily 9:30am–2pm | **Tip** Tin How Temple has an easy-to-miss entrance at the street level, so keep your eyes peeled. On the way there, take time to explore the many colorful produce and live markets that line Stockton Street.

105 Tosca Café

Still cool (thanks to Sean Penn)

One of San Francisco's greatest gossip columnists was Herb Caen, and among his favorite haunts was Tosca, a dimly lit North Beach bar on Columbus Avenue across the street from City Lights Books, just past Broadway.

On March 24, 1987, Caen wrote, "At midnight yesterday, Rudi Nureyev, the grand master of the ballet, was holding court at a corner booth in the Tosca Cafe, a place that doesn't serve food. When he said he wanted a hamburger but didn't want to go out, owner Jeannette Etheredge imported chef Willy Bishop from Capp's Corner to turn out a batch in Tosca's closet of a kitchen."

Tosca opened in 1919 and for years held a reputation as a dive bar frequented by the Beats and literati. By the eighties, celebrity sightings of all kinds were the norm, but Tosca never lost its loyalty to its locals. It was noted for its all-opera jukebox, its worn red fake leather seats, its 1920s espresso machine, its famous back room for pool and pols, and the pervasive charm of Ms. Etheredge – a welcoming and surprising character. Her circle of friends included, among others, Johnny Depp, Hunter S. Thompson, Sam Shepard, and Mikhail Baryshnikov. Bono was even inspired by North Beach Tosca to open his own short-lived Tosca restaurant in Dublin in the early 1990s.

In 2013, Ms. Etheredge owed $100,000 in back rent to the landlord and was served with an eviction notice. Sean Penn, a longtime customer, brokered a deal for two New York restaurateurs – chef April Bloomfield and her partner Ken Friedman – to buy the place. Today, Tosca has a kitchen and is listed as one of *Bon Apetit's* top ten new restaurants in America.

The original old murals lit up over the bar still take you back to the ancient ruins of Rome and the Castel Sant'Angelo. The hazy orange patina on the ceilings, left over from years of smoke-filled days and nights, is a reminder of Tosca's storied past.

106_Toy Boating on Spreckels Lake

It's anything but child's play

Every great city has a park to match. San Francisco's is Golden Gate Park, a thousand acres of Pacific splendor created in the 1870s by, among others, the Scottish horticulturalist John McLaren. McLaren took the job of supervising the park's development on one condition: "There will be no 'Keep off the Grass' signs." Such was his respect for California manners.

Nevertheless, the well-trodden park endures and also holds tight the city's past. For example, there is Spreckels Lake, named after Adolph Spreckels, a sugar and railway magnate and a quintessential San Francisco character. In 1884, he became so enraged after the *San Francisco Chronicle* accused his company of deliberately misleading investors that he shot the newspaper's founder, Michael de Young – who survived. Spreckels was acquitted of attempted murder.

At the turn of the 20th century, Spreckels, then president of the Parks Commission, built the lake at the request of members of the San Francisco Model Yacht Club, the oldest club of its kind in the western hemisphere. In 1937, the city provided funds to build an adjacent clubhouse, which contains one of the world's largest collections of antique model yachts. If you pass by and happen to spot a member coming or going, be sure to ask for a peek inside. It's a dream house for anyone interested in model sailboats, which are all made of the finest wood, with masts nearly four feet tall. Many are equipped with motors to control jib and mainsail. Members take it all very seriously. Indeed, there have been times following regattas when a sore loser has pushed a winner into the lake. Which sounds quite dramatic until you consider that the water is only three feet deep.

You don't have to be a member to set sail on Spreckels Lake: it's open to all comers.

Address 242 Columbus Avenue, San Francisco, CA 94133, +1 415.986.9651, www.toscacafesf.com | Getting there Bus: 10, 12 (Pacific Ave & Kearny St stop); 41 (Columbus Ave & Broadway St stop) | Hours Tue & Wed 5–10pm, Thu–Sat 5–11pm | Tip Try the house “cappuccino,” a bourbon-based cocktail with chocolate and milk.

Address Spreckels Drive at 36th Avenue, San Francisco, CA 94121, www.golden-gate-park.com/spreckels-lake.html | Getting there Bus: 5 (Fulton St & 37th Ave stop) | Tip A free tai chi class is offered alongside the lake every Saturday and Sunday from 8:30am to 10am. All levels are welcome.

107 Transamerica Redwood Park

Secrets of the pyramid

Since its construction in 1972, the Transamerica Building has been one of the most recognized shapes in the city skyline, and at 853 feet remains the tallest. It has 48 floors and 18 elevators, and is covered in crushed quartz, which accounts for its light color. Initially, the building included an observation deck on the 27th floor, but that was closed following 9/11. It was designed by William Leonard Pereira (1909–1985), a prolific architect in Los Angeles who was fascinated by science fiction and had a reputation for futuristic designs. The building is owned by Aegon N.V., a Dutch company.

The structure is known not only for its shape and height but also for an unusual redwood grove at its base. The trees were transplanted here from the woodlands around Santa Cruz, and continue to gain height each year. The tallest redwoods in this little green haven top 350 feet. The park is a great place to enjoy lunch while gazing skyward at the vanishing tops of buildings and trees. There are wide benches, an open plaza, flowers, and a fountain full of frog sculptures, a reference to the Mark Twain story "The Celebrated Jumping Frog of Calaveras County." Twain once worked nearby. There is something primeval about this little enclave, which is in perfect counterpoint to the steel-and-glass monolith beside it.

This park is one of more than 50 privately owned public open spaces (POPOS) in the downtown area. These include skyscraper rooftop decks (such as the one at 343 Sansome Street), sheltered atriums, walkways, and sculpture garden. These spaces were part of the "1985 Downtown Plan" and as the district grows denser with new construction, they are becoming increasingly important. They also remain among the best-kept secrets of the city. The Redwood Park is open during weekly business hours, and closed on weekends.

Address 600 Montgomery Street, San Francisco, CA 94111 | **Getting there** Bus: 10, 12 (Pacific Ave & Montgomery St stop); 41 (Clay St & Montgomery St stop) | **Hours** Mon–Fri 7am–5pm | **Tip** In the shadow of the Transamerica Pyramid stands the landmarked Sentinel Building (916 Kearny Street) with its majestic copper-green exterior. It is owned by Francis Ford Coppola, who also operates Cafe Zoetrope on the ground floor; a lovely spot for a glass of wine.

108 Van Ness Auto Row

When cars were kings

Van Ness Avenue is named after James Van Ness, who, in 1855, became the city's seventh mayor. He was best known for having tried, unsuccessfully, to stop the lynching of two accused murderers by a vigilante group called the Committee of Vigilance. Such was the city's judicial system in 1856.

Van Ness Avenue, which stretches from Market Street to the bay, served as a critical firebreak during the earthquake of 1906, and then became "Auto Row" for the next 75 years. At its height, the area was 22 blocks long and 3 blocks wide, and was filled with nearly 300 buildings devoted to car showrooms, garages, and repair shops. But in the early 1980s, high sales commissions, rising real-estate prices and an influx of Japanese cars led to the demise of the famed automotive center.

Some of the buildings on Auto Row, particularly those built in the teens and twenties, included spectacularly opulent showrooms – none more than Don Lee's Cadillac at 1000 Van Ness, now an AMC multiplex. Just inside the entrance you will still find the well-preserved lavish marble floors, crystal chandeliers, and grand staircase. It was all designed to suggest the power and grandeur of a revolutionary personal object whose engineering and design reflected the very essence of freedom and status, particularly in California.

Similar in its luxurious ballroom-like appearance was architect Bernard Maybeck's Packard showroom at 901 Van Ness. The current space, now occupied by British Motor Car, retains the dramatically tall marble columns and other original architectural elements. Down the block, at 999, the former Chevrolet dealership is one of the most beautiful remnants of Auto Row's glory days, with its Art Deco, Streamline Moderne exterior, featuring a rounded-corner exterior, a circular awning over the entrance, and an elegant black-and-yellow clock above the glass showroom windows.

Address 1000 Van Ness Avenue, 901 Van Ness Avenue & 999 Van Ness Avenue, San Francisco, CA 94109 | Getting there Bus: 47, 49 (Van Ness Ave & O'Farrell St stop) | Tip San Francisco Ballet is located close by at 455 Franklin Street. Visit www.sfballet.org to find performances that are not to be missed.

109_Vermont Street

The thrill of S curves

Vermont is perhaps the city's most anonymously famous street. It runs south from the design district in SOMA, along the slopes of Protrero Hill, past a delightful little park on the summit called McKinley Square, through a series of seven S turns – a vehicular paradise, albeit on rough cement – then jumps Highway 101 by way of a narrow pedestrian bridge and ends in the Mission District at Cesar Chavez Street.

The street has two claims to fame: It's the most crooked street in the city – the hairpins are even tighter than on Lombard Street, its manicured and better-known cousin – and it has been used in several films, notably *Magnum Force*, made in 1973 with Clint Eastwood, and *Bullitt*, made in 1968 with Steve McQueen.

In the latter, a B-movie cult classic and forever a San Francisco signature piece, McQueen plays a cynical lone-wolf cop named Frank Bullitt who becomes attracted to a femme fatale played by Jacqueline Bisset. At one point her character says, "You're living in a sewer, Frank, day after day. With you, living with violence is a way of life." And with that, McQueen is off again in his 1968 Ford Mustang, tires screeching and smoking, chasing another iconic muscle car of the era, a Dodge Charger, with bad guys in it.

That particular chase was shot in several parts of the city, particularly on Protrero Hill, but also on Vermont Street between 20th and 22nd, where the classic rules of road racing don't apply; there's no time to aim at a point on a curve and let centrifugal force bring you around. The trick is to imagine yourself as a skier carving down the mountainside, punching the brakes just like planting a pole.

Almost needless to say, it's a downhill race for the imagination only.

The more nuanced qualities of the street are to be found in the park at McKinley Square. Once there, the views of the city are compelling, particularly at sunup or sunset.

Address Vermont Street between 20th Street & 22nd Street, San Francisco, CA 94107 | **Getting there** Bus: 10 (23rd St & Vermont St stop) | **Tip** Stop at the neighborhood grocery store Chiotras at 858 Rhode Island Street for a morning latte or a delicious sandwich.

110_Wave Organ

Shhh… listen

To reach the Wave Organ, located on the end of a tiny peninsula in the Marina, you pass a grove of sailboat masts along Yacht Road and the St. Francis Yacht Club, which opened in 1927. Its members have won every great sailing race in the world except the America's Cup, which the slightly younger (by 12 years) Golden Gate Yacht Club just down the road won in 2013. The Golden Gate is newer in every sense than the St. Francis, mostly thanks to Oracle CEO Larry Ellison, whose team Golden Gate sponsors. Ellison supposedly spent more than $300 million to retain the America's Cup in one of the most amazing – and controversial – comebacks in all of sports history.

On the very tip of the jetty, you'll come to a magical spot that looks like the ruins of a Roman temple. It's the "sound sculpture" constructed in 1986 by artist Peter Richards and stonemason George Gonzales, and sponsored by the Exploratorium. The Wave Organ, a small and quaint environmental art project, reminiscent of organs in Zadar, Croatia, and Blackpool, England, incorporates cut stone salvaged from the demolition of the Laurel Hill Cemetery in the 1940s and more than 20 large plastic pipes, which emerge like periscopes from behind gray granite walls. Put your ear to the pipes and you'll catch the amplified rhythmic sounds of the tide. The unusual notes range from high to low gurgling sounds, played by the ocean as it restlessly slaps against the stones and echoes thru the tubes. This experience is multiplied in the "stereo booth," where you are surrounded by piping on three sides. The sound is best during higher tides.

The irregular terraced seating of the Wave Organ also provides an incomparable spot for a picnic, with the spectacular view of the city and some of its grandest homes overlooking what was once marshland and sand dunes, and of the bay, framed by the Golden Gate Bridge and Alcatraz.

Address 1 Yacht Road, end of the jetty, San Francisco, CA 94123, www.exploratorium.edu/visit/plan_your_visit/wave_organ | Getting there Bus: 28 (Buchanan St & Bay St stop); 43 (Chestnut St & Fillmore St stop) | Tip There are scenic running and hiking trails and bike lanes that all lead from the Marina Green to the base of the Golden Gate Bridge or over the bridge to Sausalito and the Marin Headlands.

111 Wood Line

The art of sticks and stones

The Presidio was San Francisco's original military fort; in 1776 it was the northernmost outpost of the Spanish Empire in North America. Legend has it that soldiers in the Presidio would walk inland to the Mission District to visit their sweethearts along a meandering trail that became known as Lovers' Lane. This famous trail was one of the inspirations for environmental artist Andy Goldsworthy's sculpture, *Wood Line*, a long winding string of tree trunks that snakes through a nearby clearing in an aging eucalyptus forest. The beautifully matched trunks and branches used by Goldsworthy were sourced from various tree removal projects within the Presidio.

When the U.S. Army took over the Presidio in the 1840s, they began an intensive campaign to create a dense forest on the coastal scrubland of the base's bluffs and hillsides. Eucalyptus trees were imported from abroad and planted, with native Monterey cypress sometimes placed in between them. The eucalyptus flourished, while the interspersed cypress died out, leaving long "hallways" of empty space. *Wood Line* occupies one of these barren gaps. According to Goldsworthy, the artwork "draws this space."

The story of the Presidio's forest, like Goldsworthy's work, reflects the constant interplay of man and nature along the continent's edge. Installed in 2011, *Wood Line* has already undergone transformation: the eucalyptus trunks are cracking and weathering into new patterns and textures.

A wonderful side effect of *Wood Line* are the many spontaneous Goldsworthy-inspired projects that have popped up along its path, ranging from "mini" wood lines to abstract arrangements of eucalyptus leaves. The area has become an outdoor studio where artsy types of all ages are crafting ephemeral wonders out of sticks and stones. Goldsworthy has two other sculptures in the Presidio worth seeking out: *Spire* (2008) and *Tree Fall* (2013) (see ch. 20).

Address 15 Lovers Lane, The Presidio, San Francisco, CA 94129 | Getting there Bus: 28 L, 43 (Letterman Dr & Lincoln Blvd stop) | Tip Visit the Presidio Officers' Club (50 Moraga Avenue), one of the oldest structures in San Francisco, featuring a small museum, the Presidio Heritage Gallery in the old remodeled ballroom, and the Mexican restaurant Arguello.

1
101
Sausalito
5
101
Golden Gate National Recreation Area
46
86
Golden Gate
3
2
4
80
SAN FRANCISCO
Lands End
Golden Gate Park
Lake Merced Park
3rd Street
49
Geneva Avenue
26
Daly City
280
101
San Bruno Mountain State Park
Brisbane
N
0
1.25 mi
65

2
110
28
88
Presidio Parkway
74
59
111
Divisadero Street
100
7
Lands End
55
38
California Street
Park Presidio Boulevard
Geary Boulevard
Geary Boulevard
99
91
Fulton Street
Fell St.
Oak St.
106
76
25
91
12
87
98
44
33
Golden Gate Park
71
18
Lincoln Way
7th Avenue
48
17th Street
77
92
23
72
Noriega Street
3
19th Avenue
Great Highway
Sunset Boulevard
41
Portola Drive
Sloat Boulevard
Ocean Avenue
50
19th Avenue
Lake Merced Park
N
0
0.3 mi
36

3
Alcatraz Island
39
Treasure Island
19
75
Yerba Buena Island
4
93
52
Lombard Street
Columbus Avenue
San Francisco - Oakland Bay Bridge
15
Van Ness Avenue
Market Street
64
53
Fillmore Street
James Lick Freeway
Fell St.
Oak St.
Market Street
68
85
40
South Van Ness Avenue
3rd Street
20
9
Cesar Chavez Street
32
3rd Street
79
N
0
0.3 mi

4
Bay Street
Columbus Avenue
Broadway Street
The Embarcadero
Van Ness Avenue
Pine Street
Market Street
Geary Street
Golden Gate Avenue
Howard Street
Folsom Street
James Lick Freeway
10th Street
16th Street
South Van Ness Avenue
Potrero Avenue
3rd Street
Guerrero Street
73
62
96
80
61
94
34
60
4
24
13
10
105
107
21
104
54
11
6
43
95
45
103
66
83
8
16
37
29
1
108
17
42
31
63
70
102
82
57
97
56
81
67
58
27
22
78
89
47
90
30
14
2
69
109
84
51
35
N
0
0.15 mi

Harriet Baskas, Cortney Kelley
111 Places in Seattle
That You Must Not Miss
ISBN 978-3-7408-2375-7

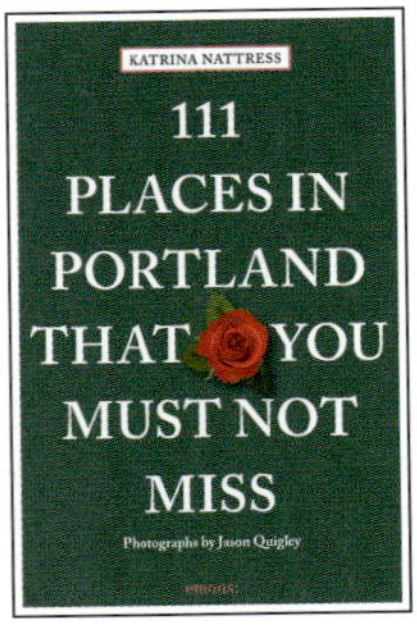

Katrina Nattress, Jason Quigley
111 Places in Portland
That You Must Not Miss
ISBN 978-3-7408-0750-4

Laurel Moglen, Julia Posey,
Lyudmila Zotova
111 Places in Los Angeles
That You Must Not Miss
ISBN 978-3-7408-2573-7

Jo-Anne Elikann
111 Places in New York
That You Must Not Miss
ISBN 978-3-7408-2400-6

Evan Levy, Rachel Mazor,
Joost Heijmenberg
111 Places for Kids in New York
That You Must Not Miss
ISBN 978-3-7408-1993-4

Wendy Lubovich, Ed Lefkowicz
111 Museums in New York
That You Must Not Miss
ISBN 978-3-7408-2374-0

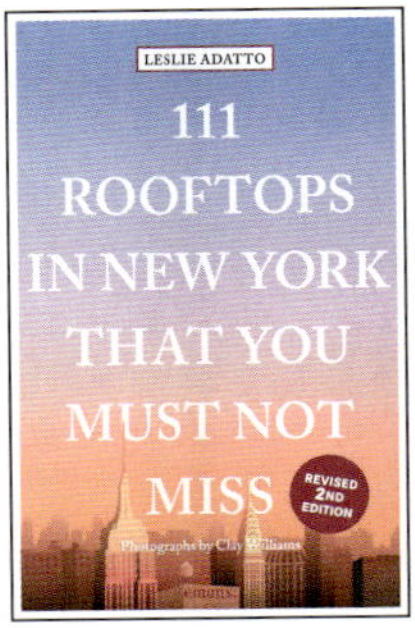

Leslie Adatto, Clay Williams
111 Rooftops in New York
That You Must Not Miss
ISBN 978-3-7408-0905-8

Joe DiStefano, Clay Williams
111 Places in Queens
That You Must Not Miss
ISBN 978-3-7408-0020-8

John Major, Ed Lefkowicz
111 Places in Brooklyn
That You Must Not Miss
ISBN 978-3-7408-0380-3

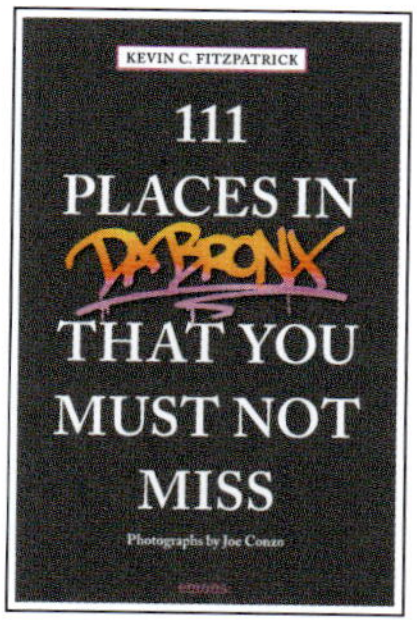

Kevin C. Fitzpatrick Joe Conzo
111 Places in the Bronx
That You Must Not Miss
ISBN 978-3-7408-0492-3

Wendy Lubovich, Jean Hodgens
111 Places in the Hamptons
That You Must Not Miss
ISBN 978-3-7408-2570-6

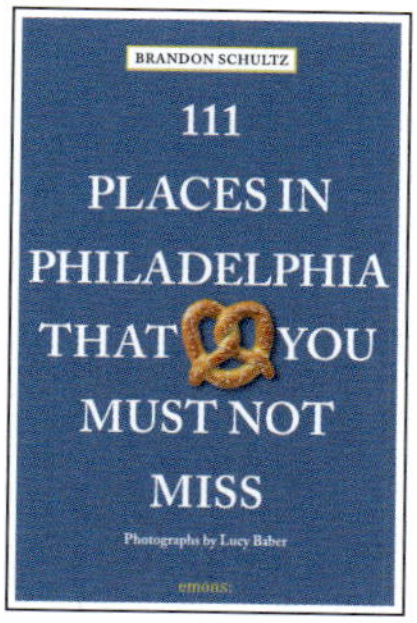

Brandon Schultz, Lucy Baber
111 Places in Philadelphia
That You Must Not Miss
ISBN 978-3-7408-1376-5

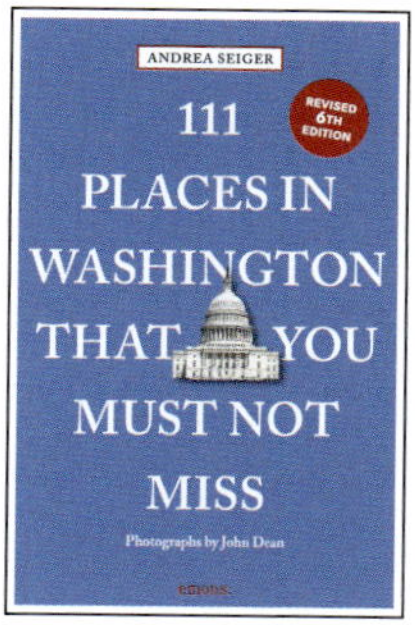

Andréa Seiger, John Dean
111 Places in Washington
That You Must Not Miss
ISBN 978-3-7408-2656-7

Kaitlin Calogera, Rebecca Grawl,
Cynthia Schiavetto Staliunas
111 Places in Women's
History in Washington
That You Must Not Miss
ISBN 978-3-7408-1590-5

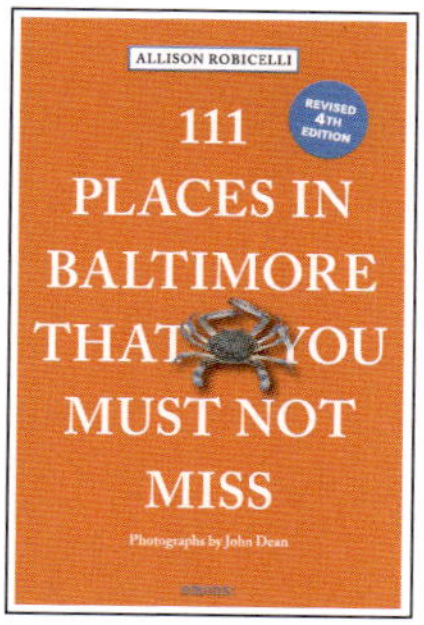

Allison Robicelli, John Dean
111 Places in Baltimore
That You Must Not Miss
ISBN 978-3-7408-2571-3

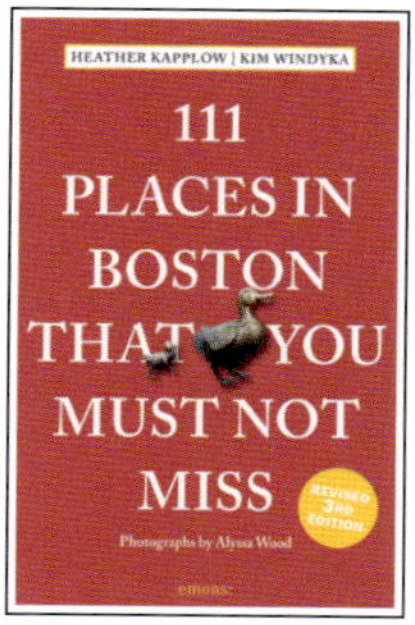

Kim Windyka, Heather Kapplow,
Alyssa Wood
111 Places in Boston
That You Must Not Miss
ISBN 978-3-7408-2655-0

Amy Bizzarri, Susie Inverso
111 Places in Chicago
That You Must Not Miss
ISBN 978-3-7408-2402-0

Amy Bizzarri, Susie Inverso
111 Places for Kids in Chicago
That You Must Not Miss
ISBN 978-3-7408-0599-9

Michelle Madden, Janet McMillan
111 Places in Milwaukee
That You Must Not Miss
ISBN 978-3-7408-1643-8

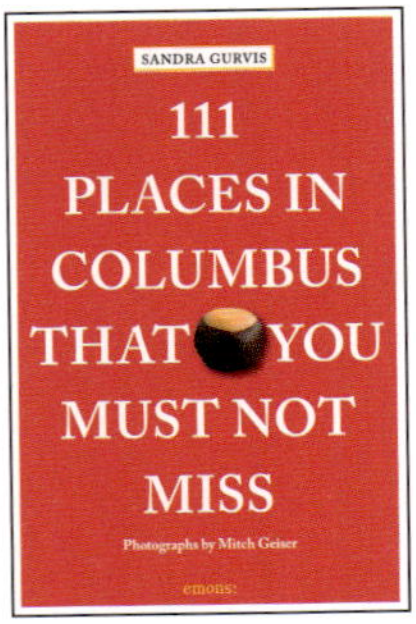

Sandra Gurvis, Mitch Geiser
111 Places in Columbus
That You Must Not Miss
ISBN 978-3-7408-0600-2

Cristyle Egitto, Jakob Takos
111 Places in Palm Beach
That You Must Not Miss
ISBN 978-3-7408-2398-6

Dana DuTerroil, Joni Fincham,
Daniel Jackson
111 Places in Houston
That You Must Not Miss
ISBN 978-3-7408-2265-1

Dana DuTerroil, Joni Fincham,
Sara S. Murphy
111 Places for Kids in Houston
That You Must Not Miss
ISBN 978-3-7408-2267-5

Philip D. Armour, Susie Inverso
111 Places in Denver
That You Must Not Miss
ISBN 978-3-7408-1220-1

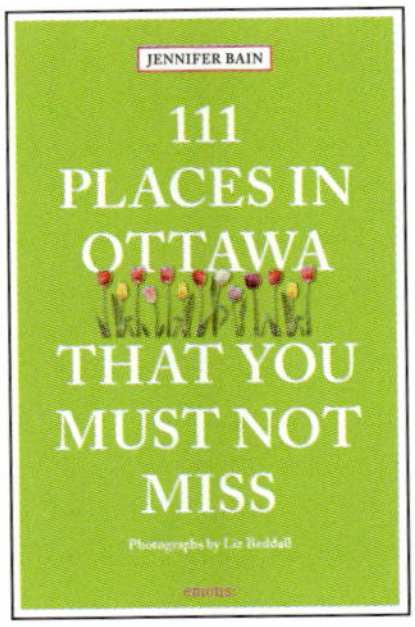

Jennifer Bain, Liz Beddall
111 Places in Ottawa
That You Must Not Miss
ISBN 978-3-7408-1388-8

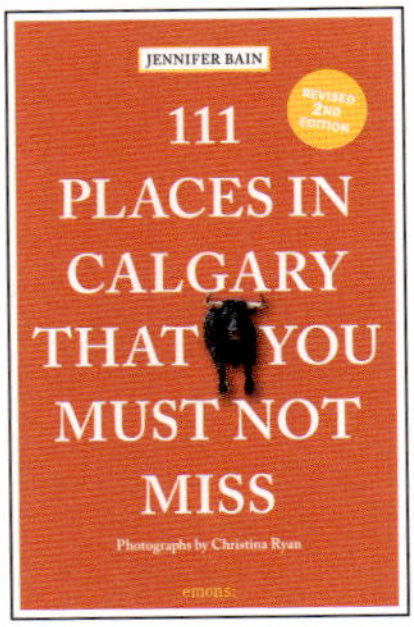

Jennifer Bain, Christina Ryan
111 Places in Calgary
That You Must Not Miss
ISBN 978-3-7408-1559-2

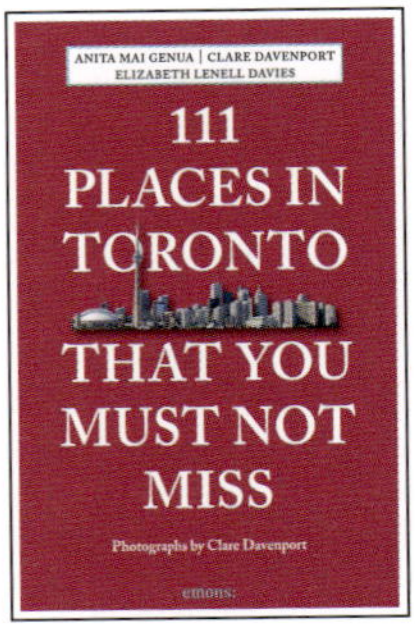

Elizabeth Lenell-Davies,
Anita Genua, Claire Davenport
111 Places in Toronto
That You Must Not Miss
ISBN 978-3-7408-0257-8

David Doroghy, Graeme Menzies
111 Places in Vancouver That You Must Not Miss
ISBN 978-3-7408-2150-0

David Doroghy, Graeme Menzies
111 Places in Whistler That You Must Not Miss
ISBN 978-3-7408-1046-7

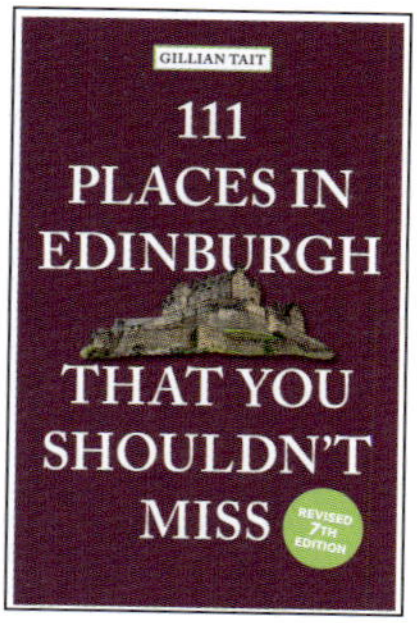

Gillian Tait
111 Places in Edinburgh That You Shouldn't Miss
ISBN 978-3-7408-2575-1

Kai Oidtmann
111 Places in Iceland That You Shouldn't Miss
ISBN 978-3-7408-0030-7

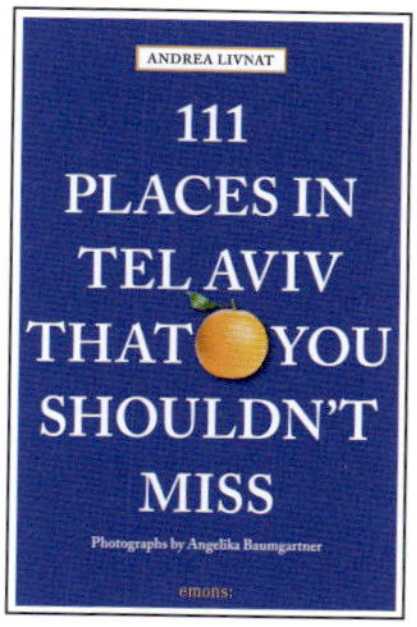

Andrea Livnat, Angelika Baumgartner
111 Places in Tel Aviv That You Shouldn't Miss
ISBN 978-3-7408-0263-9

Sybil Canac, Renée Grimaud, Katia Thomas
111 Places in Paris That You Shouldn't Miss
ISBN 978-3-7408-0159-5

Alexia Amvrazi, Diana Farr Louis, Diane Shugart, Yannis Varouhakis
111 Places in Athens That You Shouldn't Miss
ISBN 978-3-7408-0377-3

Christine Izeki, Björn Neumann
111 Places in Tokyo That You Shouldn't Miss
ISBN 978-3-7408-1277-5

Christoph Hein, Sabine Hein
111 Places in Singapore That You Shouldn't Miss
ISBN 978-3-7408-0382-7

Floriana Petersen is an interior designer with an extensive background in European art history. Her adopted and beloved city of San Francisco – with its eclectic style, never-ending capacity for reinvention, high-minded artists, and contagious joie de vivre – inspires her work and fuels her creativity. www.FlorianaInteriors.com

Steve Werney grew up in the small town of Clovis, in California's Central Valley, and has called San Francisco home since 1992. A contractor by trade, when he is not building homes, you'll find him "constructing" photographs through the lens of his camera.

The information in this book was accurate at the time of publication, but it can change at any time. Please confirm the details for the places you're planning to visit before you head out on your adventures.